WØRLD'S FASTEST CALCULATION TECHNIQUES

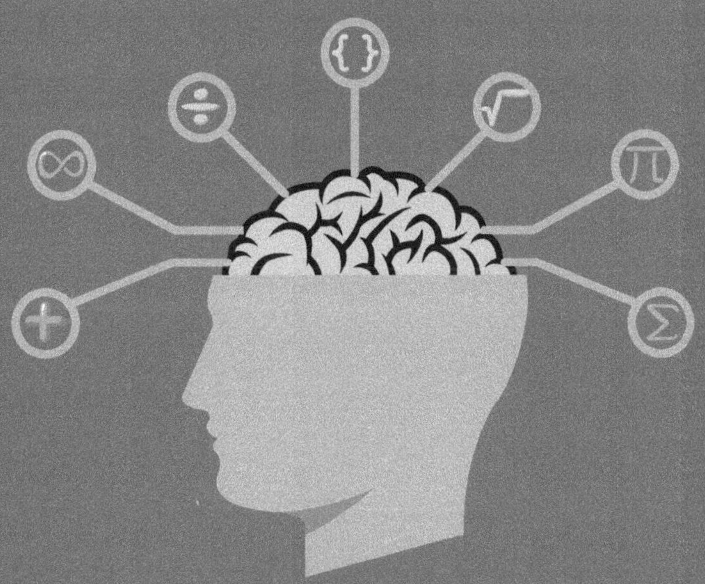

The Calculator King Vedic Maths Mastery Book
to Lightning Calculation and Amazing Math Tricks

Vedic Maths Mastery

33 **World Records Holder**

HIMMAT BHARDWAJ
Memory & Calculator King
Inventor of
Unique Memory & Maths Lab

स्वर्गीय जुगल किशोर भारद्वाज

पापा आप हमेशा
मेरी प्रेरणा के स्रोत थे-हो और हमेशा रहोगे.....

मुझ जैसे बच्चे को इस काबिल बनाने के लिए
आपका बहुत-बहुत धन्यवाद.....

आपके चरणों में मेरा कोटि-कोटि प्रणाम.....

Dedication

Dedicated to my guiding angels, grandfather, (Late) Pandit Roshan Lal, and brother, (Late) Ashish Bhardwaj. And also to my supportive and loving father, (Late) Jugal Kishor Bhardwaj. Their contribution to my life is beyond words

Dedication
Index
Acknowledgment
My Story
Introduction
13 Main Chapters

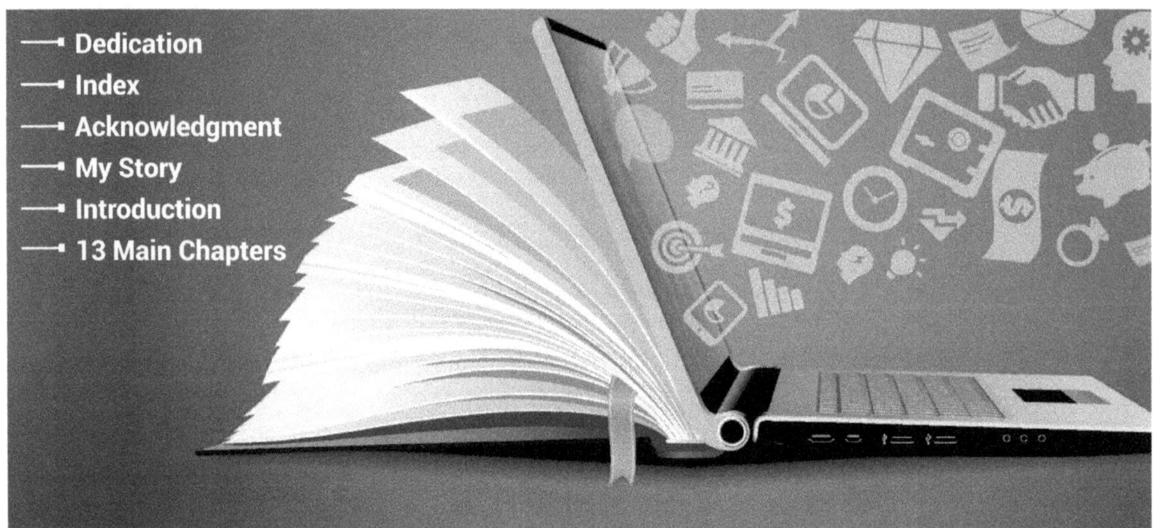

I N D E X

Acknowledgment

First and foremost, all thanks and praises to God, who blessed me with everything I need in my life. He is the reason behind all my achievements and successes. He lifted me whenever I fell, made me stronger and better with every passing moment. He loved and cared for me unconditionally. My words will fall short of describing His role in my life.

My heartfelt gratitude to Nirmal Ma'am for having faith in me. She has constantly motivated, guided, and supported me from the time I was a college student. She saw something in me that I could not see. She ignited the spark in me and helped me to become Memory King and Vedic Maths Expert.

I would like to express my special thanks and gratitude to Sagar Dodeja Sir. He is the person who has helped me in all my ups and downs and supported me at every step of my life. He has always given me things that I required without asking for any return. My journey till here was better because of him.

I want to acknowledge and give my warmest thanks to my brother, Gajanand Sharma. His presence and words always fill me with confidence and inspire me to work harder. He has always been there when I needed him. I owe him a lot.

I am highly thankful to my uncle, Shubhas Singla, who made me stand on my feet. He treated me like his own son, even without having any blood relation. He taught me the art of sacrifice, giving without expecting, and working smartly.

I owe an enormous debt of gratitude to my beautiful, caring, and understanding wife, Khushboo Bhardwaj. My heart is filled with love and gratitude for her. She is the best example of how an ideal wife and friend should be. I am extremely thankful to her for coming into my life and filling it with colors.

I am deeply thankful to Palmeichung, who helped me in finalizing this book. I truly appreciate the time and energy spent by him to provide valuable suggestions and comments. My warmest regards to him for his sincere effort.

I am immensely grateful to the editor of this book, Bhavana Vashisht, without whom my dream of finishing this book would be incomplete. She organized, edited, and wonderfully finalized this book. She is a brilliant writer and kind-hearted human. I am glad to have her on my team.

I am eternally grateful to the designer of this book, Sanjeev Saini. His hard work, creativity, and innovations completely transformed this book. He has always surprised me with his great designs. He is a gifted designer with magnificent designing skills.

Last but not least, I want to thank every reader from the bottom of my heart. Your constant showers of love and support on my online courses, YouTube videos, websites, webinars, seminars, and various other initiatives, encouraged me to write this book. I do all this for you as I want to contribute something to your life and help you achieve extraordinary success.

My Story

From Ordinary to Extraordinary

Himmat Bhardwaj
The Memory King & 33 World Records Holder

I would like to share my story with you, not to showcase my achievements or struggles but to inspire you and assure you that if I, being an ordinary boy from a remote area, can achieve extraordinary success then, you can as well. Along with 33 world records and 6 national records, I am an international memory and Vedic maths trainer, inventor, life coach, entrepreneur, and philanthropist. However, behind all my success, there is a lesser-known story full of struggles.

My journey till here has been full of ups and downs. In school, my teachers used to scold me for not concentrating on my studies. I used to get mocked by classmates. I was among those students who had exam phobia. I had no ambitions and considered studies very boring. Being a maths and memory expert now does not mean that I was good at them from childhood. Rather, earlier, they were like my enemies. I had a bad memory and hated maths. I had to struggle hard to remember details and pass my exams.

My family is from a village called Sallhawas in Jhajjar, Haryana. My father has now retired from the Indian Army, and my mother is a homemaker. From the beginning, conditions at home were not favorable, and we struggled hard to survive on less money and resources. In the board exams of the 10th class, I scored fewer marks and performed below average in maths. That generated a fear of maths inside me. Somehow, I completed my 12th class. But I was extremely frustrated. So, I quitted my studies and started selling newspapers for my livelihood. After seeing all this, my father became very sad and left everything, including his job, house, farm, etc., and shifted to Gurugram.

That acted as a turning point in my life. At that moment, I realized that I should do something for my father. I thought that my father had sacrificed everything for me, now it is my duty to make him proud. I had two options, first was to go on living a fearful, poor, and non-purposeful life, and the second was to overcome my fears and achieve something extraordinary. That was the time when I started believing in myself. I challenged the world and left behind all my fears. After that, I never looked back.

"Extraordinary accomplishments are only achieved when we are able to overcome extraordinary challenges."

This is my life story in brief. What you can take away from this story is that the journey to achieve glamorous things is filled with hardships. But there is no need to fear hardships as they come to polish you. Also, no one is born a genius. But with practice and determination, you can achieve great success. You have the power to change your destiny, and everything lies in your hands.

"Success does not happen overnight."

It takes the right amount of time, effort, sweat, smart work, and sacrifice to achieve exceptional things. Because I faced a lot of troubles, so I can very well empathize with other people. And that is the reason why I want to help everyone overcome their fears and progress in life and career.

I have included all the secrets that I used to make world records in this book. This will train you to face difficult situations and improve your overall quality of life. For you all, I will keep writing such books and keep assisting you in whatever way I can.

"Sharing is caring! The more we give to others,

the more we receive."

Introduction

Vedic mathematics is an ancient system of Indian Mathematics which contains a collection of techniques to solve mathematical problems in an exciting, simpler, and faster way.

It was rediscovered from the "Vedas" between 1911 and 1918 by Sri Bharati Tirthaji Maharaj. As per him, all of the Vedic maths is based on 16 sutras or formulae. This book contains a vivid explanation and implementation of those formulae.

Benefits of Vedic Mathematics

- Gives permanent life-long advantages
- Develops superhuman qualities and calculator in brain
- Increases calculation speed by 100 times
- Can be useful for all school, college and other competitive exams .
- Removes maths phobia
- Significantly improves accuracy
- Increases academic performance
- Boosts confidence and memory

- Acts as a powerful answer checking tool.
- Helps to develop left and right brain
- Increases problem-solving speed and efficiency
- Saves precious time
- Makes maths fun and easy
- Helps to get better results in less time
- Increases popularity among friends and other people and much more

In this Book, you will Find

- World's best maths techniques
- Systematic approach to solve any maths problem
- Highly useful and effective tips to build a strong foundation
- Reliable formulae to find answers to tricky questions related to squares, cubes, square roots, cube roots, addition, subtraction, divisibility, multiplication, calendars and many more
- Numerous solved examples and useful exercises
- Easy and interesting explanations to complex topics
- Various worksheets to give practical experience
- Colorful and entertaining presentation
- Step by step guidance to become maths expert

After Learning Vedic Maths, you will be able to

- Perform complex additions and subtractions easily
- Multiply large numbers like 2342x5432 within five seconds
- Calculate cube roots of any perfect number in no time
- Find square roots of any perfect number effortlessly
- Find the day of any date
- Check the divisibility of numbers easily
- Answer square and cubes of numbers quickly
- Calculate everything in mind without using pen and paper
- Love and enjoy maths

Now you know what Vedic Maths holds for you, enlighten yourself with some impressive secrets and powerful techniques to achieve mastery in mathematics.

It is highly recommended to complete all the examples, exercises, and worksheets' questions before moving on to the next chapter.

About the Chapter

This chapter is devoted to one of the most important and fundamental topics of Vedic Maths, which is **"Bases and Complements"**.

The chapter begins with a basic definition of bases. It then escalates to define complement and its types. Special emphasis is laid on the solution of complements to make the concept crystal clear.

The chapter contains detailed theory, which is well supplemented with well-graded illustrations and solved objective and subjective examples. Worksheets are also provided so that the students can further master these concepts.

Base — What is a Base in Vedic Maths?

Bases are numbers starting from one and followed by any number of zeros, for example, 10, 100, 1000, 10000, etc. In Vedic Maths, the base will act as a basis for our calculations.

The bases of the numbers depend on the digits of the given numbers. The **smallest base of a number is 10,** and the **largest base can be 10 raised to the power infinity.**

The base of a number simply depends on the number of digits a number has. For example, the numbers from "1-9" will have a base 10. Similarly, all the two-digit numbers (11 to 99) will share the base 100.

What do you think about 20? Is it a base? No, As it does not start with one. Similarly, 101, & between 1100 cannot be considered as bases. It is because the former ends with one and the latter has two ones.

Numbers	Bases
1-9	10
11-99	100
101-999	1000
1001-9999	10000
10001-99999	100000

Table 1.1: Numbers and their Base Numbers

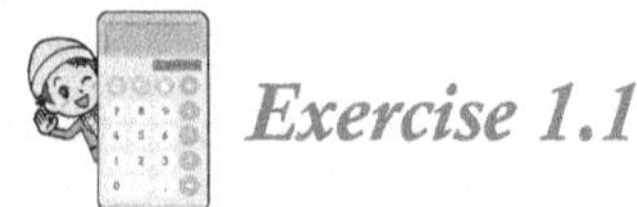

Exercise 1.1

Q1. Write the bases of the given numbers in the blanks beside them.

1)   1012 - ____

2)   2087 - ____

3)   7760 - ____

4)   1901 - ____

5)   2820 - ____

6)   9267 - ____

7)   21 - ____

8)   4 - ____

9)   73858 - ____

10)   19006580 - ____

11)   1486395 - ____

12)   234500 - ____

Complements — What is a Complement?

Two numbers that add up together to form the nearest base number are called complements of each other. Basically, they are known as complement because they "complement" or "suit" each other and together form the nearest base number. For example, as 48+52 is equal to 100, we can say that 48 and 52 are complements of each other because they add up together to form their nearest base number 100.

Types of Complements in Vedic Maths.

For the ease of understanding complements in Vedic Mathematics, they are further classified into three types:

a.   Simple complements

b.   Complements involving zero

c.   Complements of decimal numbers

Simple Complements

Simple complements are natural numbers (1 to infinite) that combine to form their nearest base number.

For example, 482+518, 56+44, 9+1, 2048+7952

Complements Involving Zeros

Complements involving zeroes are numbers that include zero either at the end of numbers or in between the numbers. If zero occurs in between a number, it will not make a difference in the calculation method.

For example, 2000, 502.30, 985006, 40805601, etc.

Although, there will be a slight change in the calculation method if a number ends with zero. We will discuss more about the method of calculation in the upcoming topics.

Complements of Decimal Numbers

Decimal numbers have always been a tough spot in our lives, and calculations involving them are considered a major challenge by most of us.

But we need to know that decimal numbers are just as simple to calculate as any other number.

Remember that a **decimal number comprises of two parts: primary and secondary. Primary** numbers are those numbers that are placed prior (or on the left-hand side) of a decimal, whereas **secondary** numbers are the numbers that are placed after (or on the right-hand side) the decimal point. For example, in 20.98, 20 is primary, and 98 is secondary.

> **Note:** The base of a decimal number will always be the base of its primary number. For example, the base number of 20.9856 will be 100 as the base of 20 is hundred.

Exercise 1.2

Q1. Put the following numbers in the column of their respective categories.

2012   8.25   39   9600   23219   5000   2   18.001   176582   99.9999
1001   280   286   157   49.268

Simple	Involving Zero	Decimal

Q2. Write the bases of the given numbers in the space provided beside them.

1)   281 _____
2)   92.2 _____
3)   801 _____
4)   9582 _____
5)   13219 _____
6)   198.256 _____

Find the Complement of a Number Quickly

A complement of a number is obtained by subtracting that number from the nearest base number.

For example, the complement of 2 is 10-2=8.

Similarly, the complement of 932 is 1000-932=68 and of 58962417 is 100000000-58962417=41037583.

The All From 9, Last From 10 Rule

Look at the subtraction problem given above; you will use a considerable amount of time if you solve them using the conventional method. Using the rule, "All from 9, last from 10", solving these questions will become a matter of fewer than 5 seconds.

> **Note:** Mostly, all calculations in Vedic Maths are done from the left to right direction.

The "All from 9, last from 10" rule states that **every single digit of a number except the last digit will be subtracted from 9 and the last digit will be subtracted from 10**.

Let's look at some examples to understand the workings of this rule.

Example 1: Find the complement of 256.

(To find the complement of 256 using the "All from 9, last from 10 [AF9LF10]" rule, we:

Step 1 - Find the base of 256.

Step 2 - Use the AF9LF10 rule for 256.)

Solution 1: S1 - We know that the base of 256 is 1000.

S2 - By applying the AF9LF10 rule for 256, we get:

9910

III

256

744

Therefore, the complement of 256 is 744.

Hence solved.

Example 2: Find the complement of 4674.

(To find the complement of 4674 using the "All from 9, last from 10 [AF9LF10]" rule, we:

Step 1 - Find the base of 4674.

Step 2 - Use the AF9LF10 rule for 4674.)

Solution 2: S1 - We know that the base of 4674 is 10000.

S2 - By applying the AF9LF10 rule for 4674, we get:

99910

IIII

4674

5326

Therefore, the complement of 4674 is 5326.

Hence solved.

> **Note:** For the numbers that end with zero(es), the last digit prior to it will be taken into consideration and will be subtracted from 10 (even if the digit prior to zero(es) is the first digit), and for the rest, the AF9LF10 rule shall apply. However, if there's a zero in between the digits, it shall be treated as any other digit.

Example 3:   **Find the complement of 180.**

(To find the complement of 180 using the AF9LF10 rule, we:

    Step 1- Find the base of 180.

    Step 2- Use the AF9LF10 rule for 180.)

Solution 3:   **S1-** We know that the base of 180 is 1000.

S2- By applying the AF9LF10 rule for 180, we get:

910

‖ |

18 0

----

82 0

Therefore, the complement of 180 is 820.

Hence solved.

Example 4:   **Find the complement of 1801.**

(To find the complement of 1801 using the AF9LF10 rule, we:

    Step 1- Find the base of 1801.

    Step 2- Use the AF9LF10 rule for 1801.)

Solution 4:   **S1-** We know that the base of 1801 is 10000.

S2- By applying the AF9LF10 rule for 1801, we get:

99910

||||

1801

8199

Therefore, the complement of 1801 is 8199.

Hence solved.

> **Note:** The process of finding the complement of a decimal number is the same. We only need to place the decimal point at its original position, i.e., right after the digits, it was placed earlier.

(To find the complement of 92.86 using the AF9LF10 rule, we

    Step 1- Find the base of 92.86.

    Step 2- Use the AF9LF10 rule for 92.86.

    Step 3- Place the decimal point correctly.)

Solution 5: b We know that the base of 92.86 is 100.

S2- By applying the AF9LF10 rule for 92.86, we get:

99 9 10

II II

92.86

____

07 14

____

S3- By placing the decimal point correctly, we found the complement of 92.86 to be 7.14.

Hence solved.

 *Exercise 1.3*

Q1. Find the complements for the following numbers.

1)   44

2)   56

3)   8521

4)   5896324

5)   50000

6)   7895

7)   7050450

8)   29.995

9)   2900.33

10)   162.25

11)   560

12)   56.6

13)   93

WORKSHEET-1

Bases and Complements

Q 1. Tell whether the following numbers are bases or not.

1)	20	2)	300	3)	6000
4)	1000	5)	100000	6)	11001
7)	10000	8)	1001	9)	5000
10)	200100	11)	2001	12)	5600
13)	4000	14)	8000	15)	10020

Q 2. Write the complements of the following numbers underneath them.

1)	44	36	22	38	13	68
2)	978	765	456	302	766	284
3)	452	308	761	859	774	623
4)	987	869	123	666	705	647
5)	7684	4656	9032	5647	1003	3777

About the Chapter

This chapter is devoted to the study of yet another important part of calculations, namely, subtraction.

The chapter begins with a basic definition of subtraction and knowledge of subtraction and further gives details of the types of subtraction in Vedic Maths. Special emphasis is given to the multiple base and number sums.

The theory in the chapter is well-supplemented with illustrations and solved objective and subjective examples. Worksheets of varying difficulty are also provided so that students can further hone their skills.

Subtraction

Subtraction is an arithmetic operation of taking the difference between two numbers. It is denoted by the minus (-) symbol.

With simple subtraction tricks discussed here, it will be just a matter of a few seconds for you to solve any length of numbers.

Types of Subtraction

In Vedic Maths, subtraction is divided into two types. Which are :

a. Mental or specific subtraction

b. General subtraction

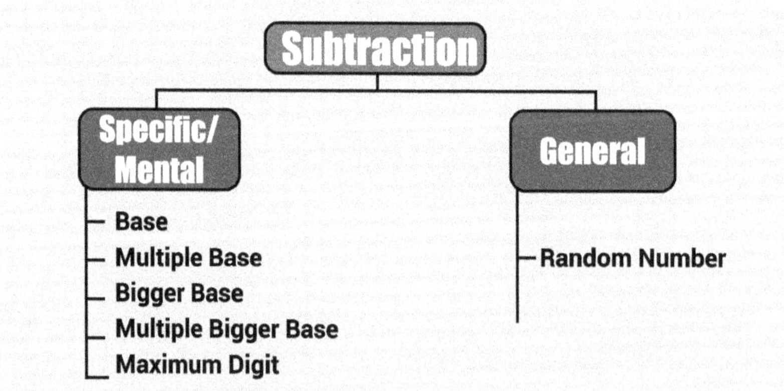

Types of Subtraction

In Vedic Maths, subtraction is divided into two types. Which are :

a.   Mental or specific subtraction

b.   General subtraction

Mental Subtraction

Mental or specific subtraction refers to the subtraction of a number from its different kinds of base. Mental subtraction is further classified into five types:

1.   Base: For example, 10000 is a base of 5884.

2.   Bigger Base: For example, 100000 is a bigger base of 5884.

3.   Multiple Base: For example, 70000 is a multiple base of 5884.

4.   Multiple Bigger Base: For example, 700000 is a multiple bigger base of 5884.

5.   Less Zeros More Digits: For example, 7000-5884 is a less zero more digits case.

Solve Mental Subtraction Easily

The Calculation of mental subtraction is mostly similar for all five types. The basic formulae you have to remember in subtraction are:

1.   All from 9, last from 10 (AF9LF10)

2.   By one less than the one before (B1LTT1B)

Since we are well aware of the "All from 9 last from 10" rule, let us now learn about the "By one less than the one before" rule.

This is a simple rule. To apply this rule, we have to **subtract 1 from the previous digit and note down the new number** (this simply means to write the number that comes before the given number).

Now let us look at some examples for better understanding.

Subtracting from Base Numbers

Example 1: **Subtract 1000-784.**

(To find the difference between 1000 and 784, we use the AF9LF10 rule for 784)

Solution 1: By applying the AF9LF10 rule for 784, we get:

9910

|||

784

216

Therefore, the difference between 1000 and 784 is 216.

Hence solved.

Example 2: **Subtract 100000-32468.**

Solution 2: By applying the AF9LF10 rule for 32468, we get:

999910

| | | | |

32468

- -

67532

- -

Therefore, the difference between 100000 and 32468 is 67532.

Hence solved.

Exercise 2.1

Q1. Subtract the following numbers:

1)   100-34=

2)   100-26=

3)   1000-34=

4)   1000-249=

5)   1000-102=

6)   10000-4252=

7)   10000-3456=

8)   100000-6100=

9)   100000-35601=

10)   10000-7100=

Subtraction from Bigger Base Number

Example 3: **Subtract 1000-28.**

(To find the difference between 1000 and 28 we:

Step 1- Add zeros before 28 to make it equivalent to the base.

Step 2- Apply AF9LF10 rule for 28.)

Solution 3: S1- Add zeros before 28 to make it equivalent to the given base.

S2- By applying AF9LF10 rule for 028, we get:

9910

| | |

028

- -

972

- -

Therefore, the difference between 1000 and 28 is 972.

Hence solved.

Solution 4: S1 - Add two zeros before 72 to make it equivalent to the given base.

S2 - By applying AF9LF10 rule for 0072, we get:

99910

||||

0072

9928

Therefore, the difference between 10000 and 72 is 9928.

Hence solved.

Example 5: **Subtract 1000000-985.**

Solution 5: S1 - Add zeros before 985 to make it equivalent to the given base.

S2 - By applying AF9LF10 rule for 000985, we get:

9999910

||||||

000985

999015

Therefore, the difference between 1000000 and 985 is 999015.

Hence solved.

Exercise 2.2

Q1. Subtract the following by adding 0s.

1)   1000-43=

2)   1000-62=

3)   10000-134=

4)   100000-249=

5)   10000000-292=

6)   10000000-252=

7)   10000000-456=

8)   100000-610=

9)   100000-356=

10)   1000000-710=

Subtracting from Multiple Base Number

Example 6: **Subtract 5000-262.**

(To find the difference between 5000 and 267, we:

Step 1- Use "By 1 less than the 1 before [B1LTT1B]" rule for 5.

Step 2- Apply AF9LF10 rule for 262.)

Solution 6: S1- Use B1LTT1B rule for 5.

S2- Apply AF9LF10 rule for 267.

Therefore, 5000-262 is 4738.

Hence solved.

Example 7: **Subtract 900000-54292.**

Solution 7: S1- Use B1LTT1B rule for 9.

S2- Now, apply AF9LF10 rule for 54292.

Therefore, the difference between 900000 and 54292 is 845708.

Hence solved.

 *Exercise 2.3*

Q1. Subtract the following sums.

1)   700-77=
2)   9000-624=
3)   5000-134=
4)   6000-242=
5)   900-92=
6)   3000-252=
7)   7000-456=
8)   80000-6100=
9)   900000-35642=
10)   200000-71009 =

Subtracting from a Bigger Base

Example 8: **Subtract 7000-28.**

(To find the difference between 7000 and 28, we:

Step 1- Use B1LTT1B rule, then add zeros prior to 28 to make it equivalent to the base.

Step 2- Add zeros at the right places.

Step 3- Apply AF9LF10 for 28.)

Solution 8: S1- Use B1LTT1B rule for 7000.

S2- Add zeros before28 to make it equivalent to the given base.

S3- By applying AF9LF10 rule for 028, we get:

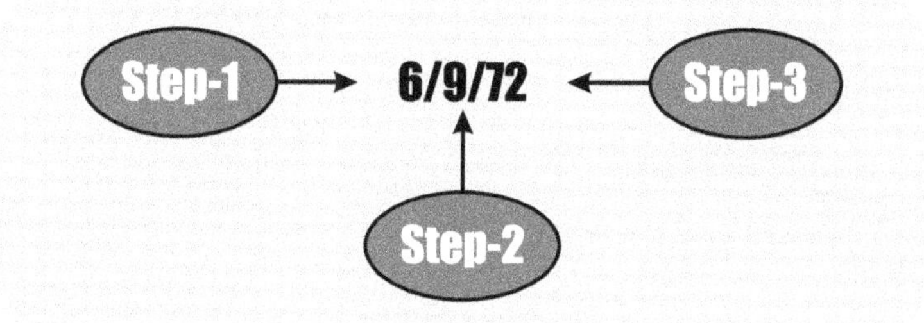

Therefore, the difference between 7000 and 28 is 6972.

Hence solved.

Example 9: **Subtract 40000-28.**

Solution 9: **S1-** Use B1LTT1B rule for 40000

S2- Add zeros before 28 to make it equivalent to the given base.

S3- By applying AF9LF10 rule for 028, we get:

Step 1 →3/99/72 ←**Step 3**

↑

Step 2

Subtracting from Multiple Base Number

Therefore, the difference between 40000 and 28 is 39972.

Hence solved.

Example 10: **Subtract 9000-3242.**

(To find the difference between 9000 and 3242, we:

Step 1- Subtract 9-3.

Step 2- Use B1LTT1B rule.

Step 3- Apply AF9LF10 rule for 242.)

Solution 10: **S1-** Subtract 9 from 3.

S2- Use B1LTT1B rule for the difference of 9-3.

S3- Now, apply AF9LF10 rule for 242.

Therefore, the difference between 9000 and 3242 is 5758.

Hence solved.

Example 11: **Subtract 8000-1254.**

Solution 11: Use B1LTT1B rule for the difference of 8-1.

S2- Now, apply AF9LF10 rule for 254.

Therefore, the difference between 8000 and 1254 is 6746.

Hence solved.

Q1. Subtract the following sums.

1)   100000-32342 =
2)   10000-624=
3)   1000000-324123=
4)   6000-22=
5)   9000-921=
6)   30000-2522=
7)   70000-456=
8)   80000-6100=
9)   900000-35=
10)   700000-71009=

WORKSHEET-2

Mental Subtraction

Q 1. Subtract numbers from the bases.

1)	100-34=		2)	100-72=
3)	100-26=		4)	100-54=
5)	1000-342=		6)	1000-643=
7)	1000-249=		8)	1000-340=
9)	1000-102=		10)	1000-549=
11)	10000-4252=		12)	10000-6350=
13)	10000-3456=		14)	10000-5400=
15)	10000-6100=		16)	10000-5103=

Q2. Subtract numbers from bigger bases.

1)	1000-32=		2)	1000-23=
3)	1000-19=		4)	1000-44=
5)	10000-47=		6)	10000-39=
7)	10000-240=		8)	10000-420=
9)	10000-23=		10)	10000-79=

Mental Subtraction

11) 10000-642=

12) 10000-513=

13) 100000-23=

14) 100000-929=

15) 100000-67=

16) 100000-812=

17) 100000-720=

18) 100000-400=

19) 1000-8=

20) 1000-29=

Q3. Subtract numbers from multiples of bases.

1) 500-23=

2) 7000-405=

3) 4000-321=

4) 6000-342=

5) 700-98=

6) 400-24=

7) 500-18=

8) 5000-555=

9) 800-76=

10) 800-46=

11) 7000-262=

12) 70000-2910=

13) 8000-342=

14) 5000-243=

15) 2000-978=

16) 900-22=

17) 50000-4352=

18) 80000-4100=

19) 7000-258=

20) 70000-6359=

Q4. Subtract the given numbers.

1) 5000-2324=

2) 90000-82454=

3) 4000-3242=

4) 8000-6743=

5) 9000-2843=

6) 700-242=

7) 2000-1254=

8) 60000-34562=

9) 6000-4360=

10) 50000-32453=

11) 7000-6244=

12) 9000-8132=

13) 900-352=

14) 300-132=

15) 500-412=

16) 60000-43254=

17) 80000-73240=

18) 7000-5452=

19) 70000-41354=

20) 8000-7643=

Subtraction Part-2

General Subtraction

In this section, we will learn the easiest way to solve the toughest subtraction problems. With this way, anyone can make world records in subtraction, just like my students and I have made.

The basic rules of general subtraction are:

1)   Buy 1 more than the one before.

2)   All from 9, last from 10.

In "Buy 1 more than the one before" (B1MTTOB) rule, we will add 1 to the given digit and put a dot over it.

Let's understand general subtraction by referring to step-by-step solved examples.

> **Note:** This may seem long in the beginning, but this is actually the shortest and smoothest method. You will realise this with an adequate amount of practice.

Example 12:   **Subtract 634258-389675.**

To subtract the numbers, we:

Step 1- Follow the conventional way of subtraction but when we encounter the first number (from which we have to subtract)<second number, then take the complement of the second number and add it to the first number.

Step 2- Use the B1MTTOB rule

Solution 12:   To subtract the numbers, we will:

S1 & S2- Use the conventional way of subtraction if first number>second number. If first number<second number, then take complement of second number and add it to the first number and put a dot over the next digit.

```
    634258
   -389675
   -----------
         3
```

We can see that, first number<second number, 5<7. Therefore we will take its complements. Complement of 7 is 3. Now, add it. And put a dot over the next number, i.e. 6 (I have coloured it instead of putting a dot)

5+complement of 7(3)=

```
  634258
 -389675
---------
      83
```

Now, we will use B1MTTOB rule for 6. We will add one to 6 and take its complement then add it to 2.

6+1=7

5+complement of 7(3)=8

Add a dot over next digit, 9.

```
  634258
 -389675
---------
     583
```

Use B1MTTOB rule for 9.

9+1=10

As 10 is a base, we will simply write the above digit, 4 as answer instead of adding or subtracting anything. Put a dot over 8.

```
  634258
 -389675
---------
    4583
```

Use B1MTTOB rule for 8.

8+1=9

3+complement of 9(1)=4

Put a dot over next digit, 3.

```
  634258
 -389675
---------
   44583
```

Having a dot over a number means adding one to it according to B1MTTOB rule. Therefore, add one to 3 and as first digit>second digit, i.e., 6>3+1, we will simply subtract it. 6-(3+1)=4

```
  634258
 -389675
---------
  444583
```

Hence solved.

Note: If you don't understand this one, no need to worry, try the next one.

Solution 13: To subtract the numbers, we will:

S1 & S2- Use the conventional way of subtraction if first number>second number. If first number<second number, then take complement of second number and add it to the first number and put a dot over next digit.

As 7<8, take the complement of 8, add it to 7, and put a dot over the next number, 7.

7+complement of 8(2)=9

```
    765467
   -289678
----------------
        9
----------------
```

As there is dot over 7, add one to it.

7+1=8

As 6<8, take the complement of 8, add it to 6, and put a dot over next digit, 6.

6+complement of 8(2)=8

```
    765467
   -289678
----------------
       89
----------------
```

As there is dot over 6, add one to it.

6+1=7

As 4<7, take the complement of 7, add it to 4, and put a dot over 9.

4+complement of 7(3)=7

```
    765467
   -289678
----------------
      789
----------------
```

As there is dot over 9, add one to it.

9+1=10

As 10 is a base, write the first number, 5 as it is. Put a dot over the next number, 8.

```
    765467
   -289678
----------------
     5789
----------------
```

As there is dot over 8, add one to it.

8+1=9

As 6<9, take the complement of 9, add it to 6, and put a dot over 2.

6+complement of 9(1)=7

```
        765467
       -289678
----------------------
          75789
----------------------
```

As there is dot over 2, add one to it.

2+1=3

As 7>3, therefore subtract 7-3=4

```
        765467
       -289678
----------------------
        475789
----------------------
```

Hence solved.

Example 14: **Subtract 846358-389765.**

Solution 14: To subtract the numbers, we will:

S1 & S2- Use the conventional way of subtraction if first number>second number. If the first number<second number, then take the complement of second number and add it to the first number and put a dot over the next digit.

As 8>5, we will simply subtract them.

```
        846358
       -389765
----------------------
             3
----------------------
```

As 5<6, we will take the complement of 6, add it to 5, and put a dot over the next digit, 7.

5+complement of 6(4)=9

```
        846358
       -389765
----------------------
            93
----------------------
```

As there is dot over 7, add one to it.

7+1=8

Take the complement of 8, add it to 3, and put a dot over 9.

3+complement of 8(2)=5

    846358

    -389765

             593

Keep following the above steps for other digits. Finally, we will get:

    846358

    -389765

    456593

 Subtract 776548-289679.

 To subtract the numbers, we will:

S1 & S2- Use the conventional way of subtraction if first number>second number. If the first number<second number, then take the complement of second number and add it to the first number and put a dot over the next digit.

As 8<9, take the complement of 9, add it to 8, and put a dot over the next digit, 7.

8+complement of 9(1)=9

    776548

    -289679

             9

As there is dot over 7, add one to it.

7+1=8

Take complement of 8, add it to 4, and put a dot over 6.

4+complement of 8(2)=6

    776548

    -289679

            69

Keep following the above steps for other digits. Finally, we will get:

    776548

    -289679

         486869

Exercise 2.5

Q1. Subtract the following numbers:

1)   98764-39856
2)   76543-28976
3)   60054-59987
4)   82454-39987
5)   54432-46958
6)   93433-33987
7)   8882214848-9213338449
8)   44567453-28976584
9)   8547965-8932569
10)   8878956-5746925

WORKSHEET-3

General Subtraction

Q1. Subtract the following sums :

	1)	91465	2)	76453	3)	84654
		-38976		-39849		-39987

	4)	76543	5)	93824	6)	84354
		-29987		-39769		-29879

	7)	65432	8)	54324	9)	33452
		-29987		-29876		-29987

Vedic Maths

10)   76453   11)   36742   12)   76543
       -39894   -29895   -29897

13)   54345   14)   66674   15)   54324
       -49897   -32987   -29987

16)   34543   17)   76543   18)   82435
       -29897   -39987   -39987

19)   98764   20)   43546   21)   93433
       -39856   -33987   -33987

22)   54432   23)   60054   24)   82454
       -46958   -59987   -39987

25)   76543
       -28976

Chapter 3a — Multiplication Part-1

About the Chapter

This chapter is devoted to the study of a very useful and essential concept, namely multiplication.

The chapter begins with the basic definition and knowledge of multiplication and discusses types of multiplication in detail.

Along with the theory, the chapter provides solved examples to give practical experience to the readers. It includes worksheets and exercises of various difficulty levels to improve the learning of students and make them practice important concepts.

This multiplication topic has been divided into two parts. General multiplication is covered after this part.

What is Multiplication?

Multiplication refers to the repeated addition of a number. It can also be understood as a product of two or more numbers. It is denoted by the "x" sign and the final answer is called product. For example, nine times nine is written as 9x9 and its product is 81.

Multiplication is often used in daily life and many people experience difficulty in multiplying big numbers. However, with this simple trick it will be just a matter of a few seconds for you to multiply any length of numbers.

Types of Multiplication

In Vedic Maths, multiplication is divided into two types. These two types are:

1) Specific multiplication
2) General multiplication

Specific Multiplication

Specific multiplication is that type of multiplication that can be solved mentally without pen or paper.

Specific multiplication is further divided into five types, they are:

1) Multiplication by 11
2) Multiplication by 111
3) Multiplication by 12 to 19

4) Multiplication by 9, 99, 999...

5) Multiplication of numbers near the bases

Multiplication by 11

The trick to multiplying a number by 11 is one of the easiest. Multiplication of numbers by 11 is further classified into 3 types:

1) Type 1- Sum of digits ≤ 9.

2) Type 2- Sum of digits > 9.

3) Type 3- More than two digits.

Type 1- Sum of digits ≤ 9

In this, the sum of two-digit numbers is either less than or equal to 9.

Type 2- Sum of digits > 9

In this, the sum of two-digit numbers is more than 9.

Type 3- More than two digits

In this, the number of digits in the given numbers is more than 2.

Type 1- Sum of digits ≤ 9

Example 1: **Multiply 32x11.**

(Here, we see that the sum digits of 32, i.e., 3 and 2 is, 5, which is less than 9; hence it falls under type 1 category. To solve such a question, we:

Step 1- First, write the ones place digit of number other than 11 at the final answer's ones place.

Step 2- Then, write the sum of both the digits at the final answer's tens place.

Step 3- Finally, write the tens digit of number at the final answer's hundreds place.)

Solution 1: To multiply 32x11, we will:

S1- Write 2 at the answer's unit digit.

S2- Add up the digits 3 and 2 (3+2=5) and write it at the answer's tens place.

S3- Write 3 at the answer's hundreds place.

We get,

3 (3+2) 2

= 352

Therefore, 32x11 is 352.

Hence solved.

Example 2: **Multiply 81x11.**

Solution 2: To multiply 81x11, we will:

S1- Write 1 at the answer's unit digit.

S2- Add up the digits 8 and 1 (8+1=9) and write it at the tens place.

S3- Write 8 at answer's hundreds place.

We get,

8 (8+1) 1

=891

Therefore, 81x11 is 891.

Hence solved.

Exercise 3.1

Q1. Multiply the following numbers.
1)   63x11
2)   72x11
3)   36x11
4)   27x11
5)   90x11

Example 3:   **Multiply 38x11.**

(Here, we see that the sum of 3 and 8 is 11 which, is more than 9; hence, it falls under the type 2 category. To solve such a question, we:

Step 1- First, write the unit digit of number other than 11 in answer's ones place.

Step 2- Then, add the digits of that number and write the unit digit of the new number in the middle (tens place) of the answer.

Step 3- Finally, add 1 to the digit at hundreds place and write it in answer's hundreds place.)

Solution 3:   **To multiply 38x11, we will:**

S1- Write 8 in answers ones place.

S2- Add the digits, 3 and 8 (3+8=11) and write the unit digit of it (1) in the answer's tens place.

S3- Add 1 to 3 and write it in the answer's hundreds place.

We get,

38x11

= 3+1 3+8 8 (the unit digit of 3+8 is written   in the final answer)

= 418

Therefore, 38x11=418.

Hence solved.

 Multiply 91x11.

 To multiply 91x11, we will:

S1- Write the 1 in answer's ones place.

S2- Add the digits, 9 and 1 (9+1=10) and write the unit digit of it (0) in the answer's tens place.

S3- Add 1 to 9 and write it in the answer's hundreds place.

We get,

91x11

= 9+1 9+1 1 (the unit digit of 9+1 is written   in the final answer.)

= 1001

Therefore, 91x11=1001.

Hence solved.

Exercise 3.2

Q1. Multiply the following numbers.

1)   78x11
2)   83x11
3)   49x11
4)   77x11
5)   95x11

Type 3- More than Two Digits

 Multiply 32542x11.

(Here, we see that the sum of the digits of 32542 is 11, which is more than 9; hence, it falls under the type 3 category. To solve such a question, we:

Step 1- First, place dots at both the ends of the number (the value of these dots is 0).

Step 2- Use the "Only the last two (OTLT)" rule. According to this rule, keep adding two digits from the last and keep noting down the sum's unit digit. Add 0 (value of dot) to the rightmost and leftmost digit and write them at their respective positions.)

 To multiply 32542x11, we will:

S1- Put dots on both ends.

S2- Apply the OTLT rule.

Starting from RHS, we get

.32542.

0+2=2

2+4=6

4+5=9

5+2=7

2+3=5

3+0=3

Therefore 32542x11=357962.

Hence solved.

Example 6: **Multiply 324672x11.**

Solution 6: **To multiply 324672x11, we will:**

S1 - Put dots on both ends.

S2 - Apply the OTLT rule.

We get,

.324672.

0+2=2

2+7=9

7+6=3 (1 carry forward to the next number)

6+4+1=1 (1 carry forward to the next number)

4+2+1=7

2+3=5

3+0=3

Therefore 324672x11=3571392.

Hence solved.

 *Exercise 3.3*

Q1. Multiply the following numbers.

1)   52324x11
2)   234324x11
3)   3124223x11
4)   2262542x11
5)   5243242x11

Multiplication with 111 is almost similar to 11. There are two minor differences in the procedure. When we multiply a number with 111, we will place two dots (instead of one) at each side of a number. Then we will apply the rule "Only the last three"; this rule is exactly similar to the "Only the last two" rule; the only difference here is that the groups formed will be in pairs of three.

Example 7: **Multiply 324672x111.**

(To find the result, we:

Step 1- Place the two dots at both ends of the number [the value of these dots is 0].

Step 2- Use the rule of "Only the last three" and add the last two digits of the number, note down their sum's unit digit and carry forward the remaining ones.)

Solution 7: **To multiply 324672x111, we will:**

S1- Put two dots at both ends.

..324672..

S2- Apply the OTLT rule for 324672.

We get,

..324672..

0+0+2=2

0+2+7=9

2+7+6=5 (1 carry forward)

7+6+4=8 (1 carry forward)

6+4+2=3 (1 carry forward)

4+2+3=0 (1 carry forward)

2+3+0=6

3+0+0=3

Therefore, 324672x111=36038592

Hence solved.

Example 8: **32423x111**

Solution 8: **To multiply 32423x111, we will:**

S1- Put two dots at both ends.

S2- Apply the OTLT rule for 324672.

We get,

..32423..

0+0+3=3

0+3+2=5

3+2+4=9

2+4+2=8

4+2+3=9

2+3+0=5

3+0+0=3

Therefore, the number becomes 3598953.

Hence solved.

Exercise 3.4

Q1. Multiply the following numbers.

1.   524312x111
2.   425343x111
3.   224214x111
4.   715322x111
5.   671332x111

Multiplication with Numbers 12 to 19

Since we know how to multiply digits by 11, let us now learn how to multiply any number with 12 to 19 numbers. This is quite similar to type 3 multiplication. The only difference here is that we will multiply the immediate left digit of the group with the digit on the unit place of the multiplier. Then add the rightmost digit of the group to it (in other words apply OTLT rule on the product).

([Immediate left digit of the group×Unit place digit of the multiplier]+Right digit of the group)

Let's look at some examples to understand better.

Example 9: **Multiply 23423x12.**

(Here, to multiply 23423 with 12, we:

Step 1- Place a dot at both corners.

Step 2- Multiply the immediate left digit of the number with the unit digit of the multiplier.

Step 3- Apply the OTLT rule on the product and numbers.)

S1- Place a dot at both ends.

S2- Multiply the immediate left digit with the unit digit of the multiplier, 12.

S3- Apply the OTLT rule on the product obtained and the original number's digits.

We get,

.23423.x12 (multiply 3x2 and add 0 [dot value] to the product)

3x2=6; 6+0=6

.23423.x12 (multiply 2x2 and add 3 to the product)

2x2=4; 4+3=7

.23423.x12 (multiply 4x2 and add 2 to the product)

4x2=8; 8+2=10 (in this carry forward case, we will write 0 and carry forward 1)

.23423.x12 (multiply 3x2 and add 4 to the product)

3x2=6; 6+4=10; 10+1=11 (1 carry forwarded from the previous digit)

.23423.x12 (multiply 2x2 and add 3 to the product)

2x2=4; 4+3=7; 7+1=8 (1 carry forwarded from the previous digit)

.23432.x12 (multiply 0x2 and add 2 to the product)

0x2=0; 0+2=2

Therefore 23423x12=281076.

Hence solved.

Example 10: Multiply 3242321x13.

Solution 10: To multiply 34434x13, we will:

S1- Place a dot at both ends.

S2- Multiply the immediate left digit with the unit digit of the multiplier, 13.

S3- Apply the OTLT rule on the product obtained and original number's digits.

We get,

.3242321.x13 (multiply 1x3 and add 0 to the product)

1x3=3; 3+0=3

.3242321.x13 (multiply 2x3 and add 3 to the product)

2x3=6; 6+1=7

.3242321.x13 (multiply 3x3 and add 2 to the product)

3x3=9; 9+2=11 (carry forward 1)

.3242321.x13 (multiply 2x3 and add 3 to the product)

2x3=6; 6+3=9; 9+1=10 (1 carry forwarded from the previous digit)

.3242321.x13 (multiply 4x3 and add 2 to the product)

4x3=12; 12+2=14; 14+1=15

.3242321.x13 (multiply 2x3 and add 4 to the product)

2x3=6; 6+4=10; 10+1=11

.3242321.x13 (multiply 3x3 and add 2 to the product)

3x3=9; 9+2=11; 11+1=12

.3242321.x13 (multiply 0x3 and add 3 to the product)

0x3=0; 0+3=3; 3+1=4

Therefore 3242321x13=42150173.

Hence solved.

 *Exercise 3.5*

Q1. Multiply the following numbers.
1.   1532x14
2.   6294x15
3.   82134x13
4.   70916x16
5.   603212x18

Calculation with numbers 9, 99, 999...

Up till now, we have seen multiplication with 11 till 19, now we will learn about the multiplication of numbers with 9, 99, 999, etc., in a very simple and time-saving way.

This category is further divided into three possible situations, which are:

oWhen the digits of 9s are equal to the number of digits of a number, like 56x99.

oWhen the digits of 9s are more than the digits of a number, like 56x9999.

oWhen the digits of 9s are less than the digits of the number, like 56x9.

When 9s are Equal to the Number of Digits

To find the product of the numbers in such cases we will use two very important concepts we have studied before, namely the concept of complements and the one less than the one before rule.

First, we will mentally segregate the final product into two parts, LHS and RHS. After dividing, we will apply the OLTTOB rule and note down the result; by this time, we will already have half of our answer. For the RHS side, we will find the complement of the number. After putting LHS and RHS together, the number we will receive will be our final product.

Example 11: Multiply 42x99.

(To solve such question, we:

Step 1 - Use the OLTTOB rule.

Step 2 - Find the complement of the number.)

Solution 11: To find out the product of 42x99, we will

S1 - Use the OLTTOB rule.

42-1=41 (this will become our LHS of the final answer)

S2 - Find the complement.

9-4=5; 10-2=8 (58 will become our RHS of the final answer)

Therefore, 42x99=4158.

Hence solved.

Example 12: Multiply 342x999.

Solution 12: To find out the product 324x999, we will:

S1 - Use the OLTTOB rule for 342.

342-1=341 (341 will become our LHS of the final answer)

S2 - Find the complement of 342.

9-3=6

9-4=5

10-2=8 (658 will become our RHS of the final answer)

Therefore, 342x999=341658.

Hence solved.

Exercise 3.6

Q1. Multiply the following numbers.
1.   19x99
2.   22x99
3.   431x999
4.   4256x9999

When 9s are More than the Number of Digits

Here, we will follow the same approach as earlier. The only change in the solution would be that for every extra 9, we will place a zero at the conjunction of the LHS and RHS. This conjunction will be named as middle (M).

Example 13: **Multiply 33x9999.**

(To solve such question, we:

Step 1- Use the OLTTOB rule.

Step 2- Find the complement of the number.

Step 3- Place 9 for every extra 9 at the conjunction of LHS and RHS.)

Solution 13: **To find out the product 33x9999, we will:**

S1-Use the OLTTOB rule for 33.

33-1=32 (32 will be our LHS of the final answer)

S2- Find the complement of 33.

9-3=6

10-3=7 (67 will be our RHS of final answer)

S3- Place 9 for every extra 9 at the conjunction (M) of LHS and RHS.

LHS/M/RHS

32/99/67

Therefore, 33x9999=329967.

Hence solved.

Example 14: **Multiply 634x999999.**

Solution 14: **To find out the product 634x999999, we will:**

S1-Use the OLTTOB rule for 634.

634-1=633 (633 will be our LHS of the final answer)

S2- Find the complement of 634.

9-6=3

9-3=6

10-4=6 (366 will be our RHS of the final answer)

S3- Place 9 for every extra 9 at the conjunction (M) of LHS and RHS.

LHS/M/RHS

633/999/366

Therefore, 634x999999=633999366.

Hence solved.

Q1. Multiply the following numbers.

1. 28x999
2. 99x999
3. 232x9999
4. 7654x999999
5. 5132x999999

When 9s are Less than the Number of Digits

Here, we will first divide the number into two; we will do this division considering the number of 9s. After the segregation, we will then add 1 to the LHS and subtract the result from the entire number. After the subtraction, we will find the complement of RHS and put them all together to get the final answer.

Example 15: **Multiply 6437x999.**

(To solve such question,

Step 1- Divide the number into two, considering the number of 9s.

Step 2- Add 1 to the LHS and subtract the result from the entire number.

Step 3- Find the complement of RHS and put them all together to get the final answer.)

Solution 15: **To find out the product of 6437x999, we will:**

S1- Divide the number into two parts based on the numbers of 9s.

As there are 3 9s, we will divide 6437 into 6 and 437 (6 will become LHS and 437 will become RHS).

S2- Add 1 to the LHS.

6+1=7

S3- Subtract the entire number from the LHS.

6437-7=6430 (this will become LHS of our final answer)

S4- Find the complement of the RHS.

9-4=5

9-3=6

10-7=3 (563 will become RHS of our final answer)

Therefore, 6437x999 is 6430563.

Hence solved.

Example 16:   **Multiply 8249x999.**

Solution 16:   **To find out the product of 8249x999, we will:**

S1- Divide the number into two parts based on the numbers of 9s.

As there are 3 9s, we will divide 8249 into 8 and 249 (8 will become LHS and 249 will become RHS).

S2- Add 1 to the LHS.

8+1=9

S3- Subtract the entire number from the LHS.

8249-9=8240 (this will become LHS of our final answer)

S4- Find the complement of the RHS.

9-2=7

9-4=5

10-9=1 (751 will become RHS of our final answer)

Therefore, 8249x999 is 8240751.

Hence solved.

Exercise 3.8

Q1. Multiply the following numbers.
1.   1234x99
2.   3222x999
3.   6358x999
4.   7598x999
5.   11456x999

Base Multiplication of Numbers

Base multiplication is the multiplication of base using base values.

The base multiplication is further divided into three categories, namely:

1.   Below the base

2.   Above the base

3.   Mixed base

Below the Base Multiplication

When the multiplier and the multiplicand both share the same base and are less than their base number, such a situation is called below base situation. For example, 92x98, here the multiplier and the multiplicand both share the same near base 100 and are less than 100.

To solve such questions, we will first take out the complement of the number and subtract any one of these complements with their opposite or cross number. This will give us half of our answer; for the rest half, we will multiply the complements with each other.

> *Note:* If the product of the complement is less than its base then we need to fill the remaining gap by adding the required number of 0s in front of the product to make it equal to their base.

Example 17: **Multiply 98x92.**

(To multiply 98x92, we:

Step 1- Take the complements of 92 and 98 and cross subtract.

Step 2- Multiply the complements together and combine the outcomes.)

Solution 17: **To multiply 98x92, we will:**

S1- Find out the complements of 98 and 92 and cross-subtract the numbers.

To get complements of 98 and 92, we subtract them from 2 and 8, respectively.

98-2

92-8

After cross-subtraction, we get, 98-8 or 92-2=90 (this will be our LHS of the final answer)

S3- Multiply the complements.

2x8=16 (this will be our RHS of the final answer)

Therefore, 92x98=9016.

Hence solved.

Example 18: **Multiply 996x994.**

Solution 18: **To multiply 996x994, we will:**

S1- Find out the complements of 996 and 994 and cross-subtract the numbers.

To get complements of 996 and 994, we subtract them from 4 and 6, respectively.

996-4

994-6

After cross-subtraction we get, 996-6 or 994-4=990 (this will be our LHS of the final answer).

S2- Multiply the complements.

4x6=24

24 is a two-digit number, but here base of 996 and 994 is 1000. So, to balance the base, we add 0 in front of 24 (024 will be our RHS of the final answer).

Therefore, 996x994=990024.

Hence solved.

Exercise 3.9

Q1. Multiply the following numbers.

1. 96x91
2. 97x98
3. 994x992
4. 9992x9996
5. 9997x9995

Above the Base Multiplication

When the multiplier and the multiplicand both share the same base and are more than their base number, such a situation is called below base situation. For example, 105x106; here, the multiplier and the multiplicand both share the same near base 100 and are more than 100.

To solve such problems, we will first observe the number and check their near base. After we know their near base, we will find the surplus of the numbers and cross-add. Then we will multiply the surplus amongst them and write them all together.

Example 19: **Multiply 105x106.**

(To find the solution, we:

Step 1-Consider the nearest base of these two numbers, find their surplus number and cross add one pair.

Step 2- Multiply the surplus together and combine them to find a final answer.)

Solution 19: **To multiply 105x106, we will:**

S1- Take the nearest base into consideration, find the surplus of the numbers from the base and cross add surplus of one and base of another.

105 and 106 both have the same near base 100.

The surplus of 105 is 5 and the surplus of 106 is 6.

 105+5

x106+6

Cross adding 105+6 or 106+5, we get 111 (111 will be the LHS of our final answer).

S2- Multiply the surplus amongst themselves.

6x5=30 (30 will be the RHS of our final answer)

Therefore, 105x106=11130.

Hence solved.

(To solve such problems, we will:

Step 1- Calculate the surplus and the deficiency of the given numbers, 106 and 98 and either cross-add or subtract any one of the pairs to get the LHS.

Step 2- Multiply the surplus and deficiency together and note the product in the RHS with a bar sign above it.

Step 3- To remove the bar, subtract one from the LHS and take complement of the RHS and combine both sides.)

Solution 21: **To multiply 106x98, we will:**

S1- Find the surplus and the deficiency of 106 and 98 and either cross-add or subtract any one of the pairs to get the LHS.

106+6

 98-2

The LHS will be 106-2 or 98+6=104.

S2- Multiply the surplus and deficiency together and note the product in the RHS with a bar sign above it.

6x(-2)=(-)12=(12)

S3- To remove the bar, subtract one from the LHS and take complement of the RHS and combine both sides.

104-1=103 (final LHS)

Complement of (12) =100-12=88 (final RHS)

Therefore, 106x98=10388.

Hence solved.

Example 22: **Multiply 108x96.**

Solution 22: **To multiply 108x96, we will:**

S1- Find the surplus and the deficiency of 108 and 96 and either cross-add or subtract any one of the pairs to get the LHS.

108+8

 96-4

The LHS will be 108-4 or 98+8=104.

S2- Multiply the surplus and deficiency together and note the product in the RHS with a bar sign above it.

8x(-4)=(-)32=(32)

S3- To remove the bar, subtract one from the LHS and take complement of the RHS and combine both sides.

104-1=103 (final LHS)

Complement of (32) =100-32=68 (final RHS)

Therefore, 108x96=10368.

Hence solved.

Exercise 3.11

Q1. Multiply the following numbers.
1.	107x98
2.	105x93
3.	1012x989
4.	1004x999
5.	10008x9996

3b Multiplication Part-2

General Multiplication

Another form of multiplication is general multiplication. As we know, specific subtraction is a very simple one-line technique, but it is limited to certain numbers, whereas general multiplication can be used for more categories.

The general multiplication is further divided into four types:

1. Two by two multiplication
2. Three by two multiplication
3. Four by two multiplication
4. Three by three multiplication

Two by Two Multiplication

This is the easiest form of general multiplication and also the fastest one. It is also known as the "IXI" method.

This type of multiplication is used when a two-digit number is multiplied by a two-digit number.

To solve it, we will first multiply both the unit digits of the number together, forming an "I" pattern and note it in the answer's ones place. Then we will cross multiply both the numbers together, forming a "X" pattern and add their product. Then again, we will multiply the digits at tens place among themselves, forming an "I". Remember, in the case of two or more-digit number, we will only write the unit digit and carry forward the rest to the next step.

Example 23: **Multiply 42x23.**

(To multiply this, we will:

Step 1 - First, multiply the unit digits [this will form I shape].

Step 2 - Cross multiply the numbers and add their product [this will form X shape].

Step 3 - Multiply the tens place digits [this will form I shape].)

Solution 23: **To multiply 42x23, we will:**

S1 - Multiply the unit digits that are, 2 and 3.

2x3=6 (6 will be our answer's unit digit)

S2- Cross-multiply the digits of 42 and 23 and add their product.

4 2

X

2 3

4x3=12; 2x2=4; 12+4=16 (6 will be our answer's tens place digit and 1 will be carried forward)

S3- Multiply the tens place digits among themselves, i.e., 4x2.

4x2=8; 8+1=9 (9 will be our answer's hundreds place digit)

So,

 42

x23

966

Therefore, 42x23 is 966.

Hence solved.

<table><tr><td>Example 24:</td><td>Multiply 63x42.</td></tr></table>

<table><tr><td>Solution 24:</td><td>To multiply 63x42, we will:</td></tr></table>

S1- Multiply the unit digits that are, 3 and 3.

3x2=6 (6 will be our answer's unit digit)

S2- Cross multiply the digits of 63 and 42 and add their product.

6 3

X

4 2

6x2=12; 3x4=12; 12+12=24 (4 will be our answer's tens place digit and 2 will be carried forward)

S3- Multiply the tens place digits among themselves, i.e., 6x4.

6x4=24; 24+2=26 (6 will be our answer's hundreds place digit and 2 will be our answer's thousands place digit)

So,

 63

X42

2646

Therefore, 63x42=2646.

Hence solved.

Q1. Multiply the following numbers.

1.   54x32
2.   44x24
3.   26x62
4.   51x43
5.   33x33

Three by Two Multiplication

This is another simple multiplication technique to multiply a three-digit number by a two-digit number. This trick is almost similar to the two by two multiplication method. Here, we will use the "IXXI" method for calculation.

In this method, we will multiply the unit digits first, forming an "I" then we will cross multiply and add the ones and the tens digit. Then we will cross multiply and add the tens digit to tens digit of the multiplier and hundred's digit to the unit digit of the multiplier and add, forming a "XX" and then we will multiply the hundreds digit with the tens digit of the multiplier, forming it an "I". We can also use dots to make this process easier.

Example 25: **Multiply 322x23.**

(To solve such questions, we will:

Step 1- Multiply the unit digits of both numbers (I formation).

Step 2- Cross multiply and add the tens and ones digits (X formation).

Step 3- Cross multiply and add the hundreds digit of the larger number to the unit digit of the smaller number and tens digit of the larger number to tens digit of the smaller number (X formation).

Step 4- Multiply hundreds digit of larger number with the tens digit of smaller number (I formation).

Solution 25: **To multiply 322x23, we will:**

S1- Multiply the unit digits of both numbers (I formation).

3 2 2

  |

 2 3

2x3=6

S2- Cross multiply and add the ones to the tens digit (X formation).

3 2 2

  X

 2 3

2x3+2x2=10 (keep 0 in the unit place and carry forward 1)

S3- Cross multiply hundreds digit with one and tens digit with tens and add their products (X formation).

322

\|

 \

 |\

 23

2x2+3x3=13; 1+13=14 (1 carried forward; keep 4 in the unit place and carry forward 1)

S4- Multiply hundreds digit with tens (I formation).

323

\

 23

3x2=6; 6+1=7 (1 from last step)

Therefore, 322x23=7406.

Hence solved.

Example 26: **Multiply 534x33.**

Solution 26: **To multiply 534x33, we will:**

S1- Multiply the unit digits of both numbers (I formation).

534

 |

 33

4x3=12

S2- Cross multiply and add the ones to the tens digit (X formation).

534

 X

 33

3x3+4x3=21; 21+1=22 (keep 2 in the unit place and carry forward 2)

S3- Cross multiply hundreds digit with one and tens digit with tens and add their products (X formation).

534

\|

 \

 |\

 33

5x3+3x3=24; 24+2=26 (2 carried forward; keep 6 in the unit place and carry forward 2)

S4- Multiply hundreds digit with tens (I formation).

534

\

 33

5x3=15; 15+2=17

Therefore, 534x33=17622.

Hence solved.

Exercise 3.13

Q1. Multiply the following numbers.

1.   544x54
2.   432x24
3.   622x62
4.   315x43
5.   232x35

Four by Two Multiplication

Four by two multiplication includes a four-digit number that is multiplied by a two-digit number. Here we will form "IXXXI".

In this method, we will multiply the ones digits first, forming an "I" then, we will cross multiply and add the ones and the tens digit. Then we will cross multiply and add the tens digit to tens digit of the multiplier and hundreds digit to the ones digit of the multiplier and add them, then we will cross multiply the hundreds digit with the tens digit and the thousands digit with the ones digit forming a "XXX" and then we will multiply the thousands digit with the tens digit of the multiplier forming an "I."

Example 27:   **Multiply 3242x52.**

(To solve such questions, we:

Step 1- Multiply the unit digits.

Step 2- Cross multiply and add the tens and ones digit.

Step 3- Cross multiply and add the hundreds and the unit digit and tens with tens digit.

Step 4- Multiply the thousands digit with the unit digit and the hundreds digit with the tens digit.

Step 5- Multiply thousands with the tens digit.)

Solution 27:   **To multiply 3242x52, we will:**

S1- Multiply the unit digits (I formation).

3 2 4 2

    |

  5 2

2x2=4

S2- Cross Multiply and add the ones and the tens digit (X formation).

3 2 4 2

X

5 2

4x4+5x2=18

S3- Cross Multiply hundreds digit with one and tens digit with tens and add their products (X formation).

3 2 4 2

\|

\

I\

5 2

2x2+4x5=24; 24+1=25 (1 from last step)

S4- Multiply hundreds digit with one's digit and thousand with tens (X formation).

3 2 4 2

\|

\

I\

5 2

2x5+3x2=16; 16+2=18

S5- Multiply thousands digit with the tens digit (I formation).

3 2 4 2

\

\

\

5 2

3x5=15; 15+1=16

Therefore, 3242x52=168584.

Hence solved.

Example 28: **Multiply 5242x33.**

Solution 28: **To multiply 5242x33, we will:**

S1- Multiply the unit digits (I formation).

5 2 4 2

|

3 3

2x3=6

S2- Cross Multiply and add the ones and the tens digit (X formation).

5 2 4 2

   X

  3 3

4x3+2x3=18

S3- Cross Multiply hundreds digit with one and tens digit with tens and add their products (X formation).

5 2 4 2

  \\|

   \\

   |\\

  3 3

2x3+4x3=18; 18+1=19 (1 from last step)

S4- Multiply hundreds digit with one's digit and thousand with tens (X formation).

5 2 4 2

\\|

 \\

  |\\

  3 3

5x3+2x3=21; 21+1=22

S5- Multiply thousands digit with the tens digit (I formation).

5 2 4 2

\\

 \\

  \\

  3 3

5x3=15; 15+2=17

Therefore, 5242x33=172986.

Hence solved.

 *Exercise 3.14*

Q1. Multiply the following numbers.

1.   4232x38
2.   4222x52
3.   5123x43
4.   3152x22
5.   2321x35

This method is very easy although, a little tricky to understand. Using this method, we will multiply a three-digit number with another three-digit number.

In this method, we will first, as usual, multiply the unit digits together (I formation), then we will cross multiply the tens digits with the ones digits (X formation) and add all of them, after that we will cross multiply the hundreds digit with the ones digit and tens digit with tens digit (X+I formation) and add all of them. Then, we will cross multiply hundreds with tens (X formation) and add the products. And finally, we will multiply the hundreds digits (I formation). We can remember the step by "IX(X+I)XI".

Example 29: **Multiply 323x242.**

(To solve such questions, we:

Step 1- Multiply the unit digits.

Step 2- Cross multiply and add the tens and ones digits.

Step 3- Cross multiply and add the hundreds digits with the unit digits and tens with the tens digit.

Step 4- Cross multiply and add the hundreds and the tens digit.

Step 5- Multiply hundreds with the hundreds digit.)

Solution 29: **To multiply 323x242, we will:**

S1- Multiply the unit digits (I formation).

3 2 3

   |

2 4 2

3x2=6

S2- Cross multiply and add the tens and ones digits.

(X formation).

3 2 3

   X

2 4 2

2x2+3x4=16

S3- Cross multiply the hundreds digits with the unit digits and tens with the tens digit and add them all. (X+I formation).

3 2 3

\|/

/|\

2 4 2

3x2+3x2+2x4=20; 20+1=21

S4- Cross multiply and add the hundreds and the tens digit. (X formation).

323

X

242

3x4+2x2=16; 16+2=18

S5- Multiply the hundreds digits together.

323

|

242

3x2=6; 6+1=7

Therefore,323x242=78166

Hence solved.

Example 30: **Multiply 523x324.**

Solution 30: **To multiply 523x324, we will:**

S1- Multiply the unit digits (I formation).

523

|

324

3x4=12

S2- Cross multiply and add the tens and ones digits.

(X formation).

523

X

324

2x4+3x2=14; 14+1=15

S3- Cross multiply the hundreds digits with the unit digits and tens with the tens digit and add them all. (X+I formation).

523

\|/

/|\

324

5x4+3x3+2x2=33; 33+1=34

S4- Cross multiply and add the hundreds and the tens digit. (X formation).

523

X

324

5x2+2x3=16; 16+3=19

S5- Multiply the hundreds digits together.

5 2 3

|

3 2 4

5x3=15; 15+1=16

Therefore, 523x324=169452

Hence solved.

Exercise 3.15

Q1. Multiply the following numbers.

1.   523x422
2.   313x292
3.   261x135
4.   412x312
5.   333x411

WORKSHEET-4

Magic with 11 (Type-1, 2)

1. **Multiply by 11 and write the answers only :**

1) 22 × 11 =	2) 90 × 11 =	3) 33 × 11 =
4) 43 × 11 =	5) 71 × 11 =	6) 34 × 11 =
7) 72 × 11 =	8) 63 × 11 =	9) 25 × 11 =
10) 81 × 11 =	11) 45 × 11 =	12) 53 × 11 =
13) 70 × 11 =	14) 81 × 11 =	15) 60 × 11 =

Magic with 11 (Type-3)

2. **Multiply by 11 and write the answers only :**

1) 722 × 11 =	2) 125 × 11 =	3) 623 × 11 =

4) $832 \times 11 =$ 5) $6014 \times 11 =$ 6) $1532 \times 11 =$

7) $7224 \times 11 =$ 8) $7232 \times 11 =$ 9) $82134 \times 11 =$

10) $70916 \times 11 =$

3. Multiplication by 12-19
   Multiply the following sums :

1) $34523 \times 12 =$ 2) $64324 \times 12 =$

3) $62586 \times 12 =$ 4) $345542 \times 12 =$

5) $41432 \times 13 =$ 6) $842621 \times 13 =$

7) $22144 \times 13 =$ 8) $342214 \times 14 =$

9) $62512 \times 14 =$ 10) $712243 \times 14 =$

11) $314251 \times 15 =$ 12) $5243 \times 15 =$

13) $54338 \times 15 =$ 14) $6424 \times 16 =$

15) $323 \times 17 =$ 16) $23421 \times 18 =$

17) $416 \times 18 =$ 18) $532 \times 18 =$

19) $2561 \times 19 =$ 20) $23051 \times 19 =$

4. 2×2 Multiplication

1) $\begin{array}{r} 3\ 4 \\ \times\ 6\ 2 \\ \hline \\ \hline \end{array}$ 2) $\begin{array}{r} 4\ 6 \\ \times\ 2\ 4 \\ \hline \\ \hline \end{array}$ 3) $\begin{array}{r} 8\ 6 \\ \times\ 2\ 6 \\ \hline \\ \hline \end{array}$

4) $\begin{array}{r} 2\ 3 \\ \times\ 2\ 6 \\ \hline \\ \hline \end{array}$ 5) $\begin{array}{r} 7\ 1 \\ \times\ 2\ 9 \\ \hline \\ \hline \end{array}$ 6) $\begin{array}{r} 3\ 4 \\ \times\ 6\ 3 \\ \hline \\ \hline \end{array}$

7) 7 0 × 7 4 ------ ------	8) 6 4 × 7 2 ------ ------	9) 2 2 × 4 3 ------ ------
10) 6 5 × 7 2 ------ ------	11) 4 5 × 5 6 ------ ------	12) 9 2 × 3 4 ------ ------
13) 3 9 × 4 2 ------ ------	14) 3 3 × 2 2 ------ ------	15) 6 4 × 7 5 ------ ------
16) 8 8 × 2 2 ------ ------	17) 4 6 × 2 6 ------ ------	18) 5 6 × 5 3 ------ ------
19) 7 3 × 7 4 ------ ------	20) 8 4 × 7 4 ------ ------	

5. 3 × 2 Multiplication

1) 2 1 3 × 2 3 ------- -------	2) 3 2 6 × 3 5 ------- -------	3) 1 2 5 × 2 8 ------- -------
4) 3 2 0 × 1 2 ------- -------	5) 1 2 2 × 3 2 ------- -------	6) 4 0 4 × 2 1 ------- -------

7) 4 1 3	8) 2 4 5	9) 1 2 5
× 1 3	× 3 4	× 1 4

10) 3 2 3	11) 1 3 7	12) 2 4 3
× 2 5	× 6 3	× 2 4

13) 3 2 2	14) 4 1 7	15) 1 2 7
× 2 6	× 4 5	× 4 3

16) 3 0 5	17) 4 8 3	18) 2 6 4
× 2 5	× 1 2	× 5 5

19) 5 6 9	20) 2 6 4
× 3 6	× 8 2

6.   4 × 2 Multiplication

1) 3 7 1 5	2) 4 6 9 7	3) 6 4 8 2
× 2 4	× 3 5	× 2 4

4) 4 7 3 1	5) 1 4 2 6	6) 2 6 3 3
× 6 3	× 2 6	× 4 5

7)   9 1 5 0
     ×   2 8
 ---------- 	
 ---------- 	
	8) 8 5 7 2
	     × 3 4
	 ---------- 	
	 ---------- 	
		9) 6 2 3 4
		     × 6 2
		 ---------- 	
		 ---------- 	

10)   2 3 6 4
     ×   8 3
 ---------- 	
 ---------- 	
	11) 3 6 4 2
	     × 5 5
	 ---------- 	
	 ---------- 	
		12) 3 2 4 3
		     × 7 2
		 ---------- 	
		 ---------- 	

13)   8 7 4 2
     ×   8 3
 ---------- 	
 ---------- 	
	14) 8 7 4 2
	     × 3 3
	 ---------- 	
	 ---------- 	
		15) 7 6 5 4
		     × 4 2
		 ---------- 	
		 ---------- 	

16)   5 4 7 2
     ×   6 2
 ---------- 	
 ---------- 	
	17) 3 3 5 4
	     × 2 3
	 ---------- 	
	 ---------- 	
		18) 4 4 5 2
		     × 3 5
		 ---------- 	
		 ---------- 	

19)   4 5 2 4
     ×   2 3
 ---------- 	
 ---------- 	
	20) 9 2 5 3
	     × 6 2
	 ---------- 	
	 ---------- 		

7.   3 × 3 Multiplication

1) 2 1 9 × 3 2 2 -------- --------	2) 4 2 2 × 1 3 6 -------- --------	3) 2 1 1 × 4 8 2 -------- --------
4) 3 2 8 × 1 1 6 -------- --------	5) 1 1 7 × 2 1 3 -------- --------	6) 3 2 9 × 2 0 9 -------- --------

7) 3 8 3	8) 3 2 9	9) 1 5 2
× 4 4 0	× 1 2 2	× 2 2 8
--------	--------	--------
--------	--------	--------

10) 4 0 8	11) 2 2 7	12) 1 0 9
× 1 2 8	× 3 8 1	× 2 0 8
--------	--------	--------
--------	--------	--------

13) 1 2 8	14) 2 9 9	15) 5 1 9
× 2 8 1	× 2 1 1	× 1 8 6
--------	--------	--------
--------	--------	--------

16) 1 2 7	17) 2 2 7	18) 3 7 1
× 2 9 9	× 3 9 0	× 1 8 7
--------	--------	--------
--------	--------	--------

19) 3 8 2	20) 3 9 9
× 4 2 3	× 2 2 5
--------	--------
--------	--------

8. MULTIPLICATION WITH 99999...

IN LESS THAN 4 SECONDS

Type -1

1) 888 × 999 =   2) 459 × 999 =

3) 9999 × 9999 =   4) 6748 × 9999 =

5) 707 × 999 =   6) 859 × 999 =

7) 780 × 999 =   8) 999 × 440 =

9) $8800 \times 9999 =$ 10) $8709 \times 9999 =$

11) $4350 \times 9999 =$ 12) $6705 \times 9999 =$

13) $6793 \times 9999 =$ 14) $3892 \times 9999 =$

15) $3648 \times 9999 =$ 16) $7659 \times 9999 =$

17) $999 \times 624 =$ 18) $324 \times 999 =$

19) $9999 \times 3248 =$ 20) $7647 \times 9999 =$

9.   MULTIPLICATION WITH 99999...

IN LESS THAN 4 SECONDS

Type -2

1) $32 \times 9999 =$ 2) $76 \times 9999 =$

3) $44 \times 9999 =$ 4) $89 \times 9999 =$

5) $56 \times 9999 =$ 6) $58 \times 9999 =$

7) 343×99999 8) $748 \times 99999 =$

9) $843 \times 99999 =$ 10) $442 \times 99999 =$

10.   MULTIPLICATION WITH 99999...

IN LESS THAN 4 SECONDS

Type -3

1) $345 \times 99 =$ 2) $192 \times 99 =$

3) $899 \times 99 =$ 4) $367 \times 99 =$

5) $8499 \times 99 =$ 6) $9345 \times 999 =$

7) $2514 \times 999 =$ 8) $5199 \times 999 =$

9) $3498 \times 99 =$ 10) $24850 \times 999 =$

11. MULTIPLICATION OF ANY NUMBER By 111

1)   435 x 111 =   2)   21 x 111 =

3)   7152 x 111 =   4)   2363 x 111 =

5)   3154 x 111 =   6)   3427 x 111 =

7)   2244 x 111 =   8)   54332 x 111 =

9)   3246 x 111 =   10) 7811 x 111 =

12. Multiplications by Base Method

Multiply the following numbers by base method :

1) 9 1	2) 9 6	3) 9 8	4) 8 6
× 9 8	× 9 3	× 8 8	× 9 8

5) 9 9 7	6) 9 9 8	7) 9 8 9	8) 9 9 6
× 9 9 3	× 9 9 4	× 9 9 8	× 9 8 9

9) 9901	10) 9997	11) 9998	12) 9999
× 9989	× 9901	× 9991	× 9993

13. Multiply the following numbers by base method :

1) 1 0 8	2) 1 0 3	3) 1 0 9	4) 1 0 6
× 1 0 9	× 1 0 4	× 1 0 2	× 1 0 4

5) 1 0 1 2	6) 1 0 1 3	7) 1 0 0 7	8) 1 0 0 3
× 1 0 0 1	× 1 0 0 4	× 1 0 0 8	× 1 0 0 2

13. Multiply the following numbers by base method :

9) 1006	10) 1009	11) 1004	12) 1003
× 1012	× 1012	× 1008	× 1002

13. Multiply the following numbers by base method :

1) 1 0 4	2) 9 3	3) 8 9	4) 1 0 1
× 9 8	× 1 0 7	× 1 0 2	× 9 7

5) 1 1 2	6) 1 0 8	7) 1 0 0 4	8) 1 0 0 9
× 9 5	× 9 2	× 9 8 8	× 9 8 9

9) 997	10) 1009	11) 1008	12) 1001
× 1007	× 994	× 906	× 905

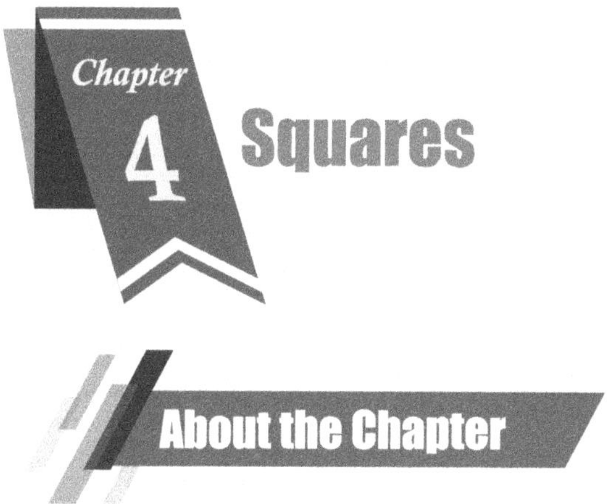

Squares

About the Chapter

This chapter is devoted to the study of another essential part of calculations, namely squares.

This chapter begins with the basic definition and knowledge of squares. For ease of understanding, squares are divided into two parts: general and specific. Special emphasis is laid on the specific type of squares.

The theory is complemented with nice illustrations and solved examples. Exercises and worksheets are also provided for the benefit of students.

What are Squares?

Square is the result obtained after multiplying a number by itself. For example, the square number of 2 is 2x2 that is 4. Similarly, the square number of 13 is 13x13 that is 169.

Generally, we are advised to memorize the square numbers, but this advice is not practical as there are infinite numbers and the chances of confusion are quite high.

Therefore, to avoid such mistakes, we tend to calculate the squares of a number by direct multiplication technique, which is a very time consuming and lengthy process. That's why it is important to learn some shortcut techniques that can save our time and give us accurate solutions.

In Vedic Maths, the techniques to find squares of a number are divided into two categories, namely, general and specific. The general technique can help us in all situations, whereas the specific technique can give us answers to specific types of numbers without using pen and paper.

General Squares

The general squares method is used to easily find out the square number or the perfect square of any number.

Here, we'll learn to find the perfect squares of a two-digit number. To find the perfect square of a two-digit number, we will first take out the square of the unit digit and note down its unit digit, and the tens' digit carried forward. Then, we will multiply the digits with each other, double the product, and again note down the unit digit, and apply the carry forward rule. Then, we will take out the square of the tens digit and apply the carry forward rule and note it down.

Let us look at some examples to understand the topic well.

Example 1: **Find the square of 33.**

(To find the square number of 33, we:

Step 1- Take the square of the unit digit.

Step 2- Multiply the digits together and double them.

Step 3- Take the square of the tens digit number.)

Solution 1: **To find the square of 33, we will:**

S1- Take the square of the unit digit (3).

The square of 3 will be 3x3, that is 9.

S2- Then multiply the digits among themselves and double their product.

So, 3x3=9 and 9x2=18.

As 18 is a two-digit number, we will carry forward 1 of 18.

S3- Finally, find the square of the tens digit (3 of 33).

The square of the tens digit is 3x3=9.

From the result of S2, we will add the carried forward 1 of 18 to the result of S3 (9) and write the output (10) on the RHS, and we will write 8 of 18 along with S1 result on the LHS side.

So, the square number of 33 becomes 1089.

Hence solved.

Example 2: **Find the square of 42.**

(To find the square number of 42, we:

Step 1- Take the square of the unit digit.

Step 2- Multiply the digits together and double them.

Step 3- Take the square of the tens digit number.)

Solution 2: **To find the square of 42, we will**

S1- Take the square of the unit digit (2).

The square of 2 will be 2x2, that is 4.

S2- Then multiply the digits among themselves and double their product.

So, 4x2=8 and 8x2=16.

As 16 is a two-digit number, we will carry forward 1 of 16.

S3- Finally, find the square of the tens digit (4 of 42).

The square of the tens digit is 4x4=16.

From the result of S2, we will add the carried forward 1 of 16 to the result of S3 (16) and write the output (17) on the RHS, and we will write 6 of 16 along with S1 result on the LHS side.

So, the square number of 42 becomes 1764.

Hence solved.

Example 3: **Find the square of 72.**

Solution 3: **To find the square of 72, we will**

S1- Take the square of the unit digit (2).

The square of 2 will be 2x2, that is 4.

S2- Then multiply the digits among themselves and double their product.

So, 7x2=14 and 14x2=28.

As 28 is a two-digit number, we will carry forward 2 of 28.

S3- Finally, find the square of the tens digit (7 of 72).

The square of the tens digit is 7x7=49.

From the result of S2, we will add the carried forward 2 of 28 to the result of S3 (49) and write the output (51) on the RHS and we will write 8 of 28 along with S1 result on the LHS side.

So, the square number of 72 becomes 5184.

Hence solved.

 *Exercise 4.1*

Q1. Find the squares of the following numbers.

1) $45^2=$

2) $62^2=$

3) $73^2=$

4) $34^2=$

5) $82^2=$

Specific Squares

Specific squares technique is a quick way to find squares of specific numbers.

The ranges of those specific numbers are:

        51 to 60

        11 to 20

        40 to 50

        61 to 70

51 to 60

To find the squares of numbers from 51 to 59, we will first take the golden number that is 25. Then, we will add our golden number to the unit digit and write their sum as LHS. Then, we will find the square of the unit digit and write it on the RHS of the answer.

Example 4:   **Find the square number of 52.**

(To find the square number of 52, we will:

Step 1- First add its unit digit to the golden number and write it on the LHS.

Step 2- Find the square of the unit digit and write it on the RHS.

Make sure to balance the RHS with the base.)

Note: The rule of adding a zero prior to the RHS will always remain valid.

 To find the square of 52, we will:

S1- Add the golden number 25 to the unit digit.

So, from 52 take the unit digit, i.e., 2 and add to 25

25+2=27 (LHS)

S2- Find the square of the unit digit and write it at the RHS. Use the zero rule if necessary.

Square of the unit digit, 2 is 2x2=4

Put a 0 before the RHS (4) to balance it.

Therefore, the number becomes 2704.

Hence solved.

Exercise 4.2

Q1. Find the squares of the following numbers (51 to 60).

1) $56^2=$

2) $58^2=$

3) $53^2=$

4) $59^2=$

5) $51^2=$

11 to 20

To calculate the square of numbers from 11 to 20, we will first add the unit digit to the entire number. This will give us our LHS. Then, we will square the unit digit. This will give us our RHS. After combining both of them together we will get our answer.

Example 5: **Find the square number of 13.**

(To find the square number of 13, we:

Step 1- First add the unit digit to the number and note it in the LHS.

Step 2- Find the square of the unit digit.)

Solution 5: **To find the square of 13, we will**

S1- Add the unit digit (3) to the entire number and note its sum as LHS.

So, 13+3=16

S2- Take the square of the unit digit (3) and note it on the RHS.

3x3=9

Therefore, the square number of 13 is 169.

Hence solved.

Note: The rule of adding a zero prior to the RHS will always remain valid.

Q1. Find the squares of the following numbers (11 to 20).

1) $12^2=$

2) $18^2=$

3) $14^2=$

4) $19^2=$

5) $11^2=$

40 to 50

To calculate the square of numbers from 40 to 50, first for the LHS, we will subtract the given number from 50 and then subtract their difference from the golden number 25. Then, for the RHS we will take the square of the initial difference which we took of the number and fifty. Finally, we will balance the base and RHS correctly.

Example 6:   **Find the square of 48.**

(To find the square of the given number (48), we:

Step 1- First subtract 48 from 50.

Step 2- Subtract their difference from 25, giving us the LHS.

Step 3- Find the square of the initial difference of the number we got from subtracting with 50 to get the RHS and finally balance the RHS and the base if required.)

Solution 6:   **To find the square of 48, we will:**

S1- Subtract 50-48.

So, 50-48=2

S2- Subtract their difference with the golden number 25.

25-2=23

S3- Multiply the difference of 50-48 and balance the base if required.

2x2=4

We got 234, but we need to balance the base for 4.

Therefore, after balancing the base, the number becomes 2304.

Hence solved.

Q1. Find the Squares of the following numbers (40 to 50):

1) $47^2=$

2) $45^2=$

3) $41^2=$

4) $46^2=$

5) $43^2=$

61 to 70

To calculate the square of any number between 61-70, we will subtract 50 from the number and add 25 (the golden number) to the difference, giving us the LHS. Now, for the RHS, we will find the square of the initial difference we got from subtracting 50 to the number and use the carry forward rule if the product is more then the base of the RHS.

Example 7: Find the square of 67.

(To find the square of the given number (67), we:

Step 1- Subtract 50 from 67.

Step 2- Add their difference to 25, giving us the LHS.

Step 3- Find the square of the initial difference of the number we got from subtracting with 50 to get the RHS and then balance the RHS and the base if required.

Carry forward rule will also apply to balance the base.)

Solution 7: To find the square of 67, we:

S1- Subtract 67-50.

So,

67-50=17

S2- Add their difference to 25.

17+25=42 (LHS)

S3- Find the square of the initial difference and balance the base.

17x17=289

As the base of the RHS in this case should be 100, so we will keep 89 in the answer and carry forward 2 to the LHS.

In this way, we get, 42+2=44.

Therefore, the square number of 67 is 4489.

Hence solved.

Exercise 4.5

Q1. Find the squares of the following numbers (60 to 70).

1) $62^2=$

2) $68^2=$

3) $63^2=$

4) $66^2=$

5) $65^2=$

WORKSHEET-5

Q 1. Find the squares of the following random numbers.

1) $22^2 =$

2) $61^2 =$

3) $44^2 =$

4) $26^2 =$

5) $64^2 =$

6) $43^2 =$

7) $67^2 =$

8) $73^2 =$

9) $69^2 =$

10) $82^2 =$

Q 2. Choose the correct squares of the given numbers.

1) 85^2

a) 7125   b) 7215   c) 7225

2) 37^2

a) 1369   b) 1359   c) 1639

3) 60^2

a) 3600   b) 360   c) 36000

4) 59^2

a) 3418   b) 3481   c) 3148

5) 77^2

a) 5299   b) 5909   c) 5929

5a Magical Calendar Part-1

About the Chapter

This chapter is devoted to the study of a topic common in day-to-day life, namely the calendar.

This chapter begins with the basic definition and knowledge of calendars. The chapter is written in such a way that the learner will be able to find out the day for any date easily. Special emphasis is laid on finding the calendar days of the past two decades.

Along with theory, useful illustrations and solved examples are also given. Worksheets and exercises are also provided to help students improve their concepts.

Calendar

A calendar is a record book of dates, usually of a specific year.

Questions from calendar topic are asked in almost all competitive exams like UPSC, SSC, CDSE, etc. It becomes very time-consuming and difficult for students to solve the questions related to calendars. But with the right technique, it becomes very easy to solve any calendar question within seconds. I have made a world record based on the calendar and prepared an unlimited years calendar. Here, I will share useful secrets to become a human calendar.

Right Way to Solve a Calendar

In brief, to solve a question related to calendar, we will first look at the date given to us. Then, we will segregate the dates into three parts, i.e., date, month, and year. After that, we will encode all the three parts; then, we will add the codes together and finally decode their sum for the final answer.

Therefore, to get desired results, for the date part, we will divide the date by 7 (number of days in a week) and write the remainder as the code. Then we will move to the month part of the date. Then we will encode the year part of the entire date. After that, we will add the codes of all three parts to get our encoded answer. That encoded answer will then be decoded to get our final results. Some of the codes for dates are given in the tables below for your reference. Remember that the codes for dates are the remainder obtained after dividing the date by 7.

Date	Code
1	1
2	2
4	4
7	0
10	3
13	6
16	2
25	4

Table 5.1- Some dates and their codes.

Codes for Months

There are specific codes for months that we need to remember. Rather than rote learning, we will use memory tricks to remember them. First, read out all the codes. Then we will memorize the codes by associating them with each other. Like code for January is 1, and January is the first month of the year, this is how we can remember its code. Code for February is 4, and we know leap year comes after 4 years, and days in February varies during that period. March and February have the same codes. April's code is 0, and 1st April is considered as April fool's day, and fools can be compared to zero. May's code is 2, and if we pronounce them together, they sound like me too. June's code is 5, and this can be remembered by saying Juno has 5 juu (hair lice).

July's code is 0, and July sounds like zoo and loo both have o in them which looks like zero. August's code is 3, and 15th August is India's Independence Day and tricolour (3 colours) flags play a major role at that time. September's code is 6, and both September and six start with s. October's code is 1, and both October and one starts with o. November's code is 4, and if we put two bars on N then it will look like roman 4. December's code is 6, and half of the total number of months is 6. This is how we can remember all codes. I have shared many more memory tricks in a structured way in my book, Extraordinary Memory—Your Secret Guide to a Super Memory. You can refer to it to learn more secret memory techniques.

Month	Code	Month	Code	Month	Code	Month	Code
January	1	April	0	July	0	October	1
February	4	May	2	August	3	November	4
March	4	June	5	September	6	December	6

Table 5.2- Months and their codes

Day	Code
Sunday	1
Monday	2
Tuesday	3
Wednesday	4
Thursday	5
Friday	6
Saturday	7,0

Table 5.4- Days and their codes

2020 Year Calendar

We know the codes for days and months. Now, we will look at the 2020 calendar to understand how to find the day if a date is given. 2020 is a leap year. We need to remember that the code for the year 2020 is 2 for January and February and 3 for March to December months. Now, let's look at a few examples to understand better how to solve these calendar-related questions.

Example 1: What was the day on 14th March 2020?

(To find the day, we:

Step 1- Encode the date, month, and year.

Step 2- Add all the three encodes.

Step 3- Decode the sum.)

Solution 1: To find the day on 14th March 2020, we will:

S1- Encode the date, month and year (Notice that 2020 is a leap year).

S2- Add all three encodes.

S3- Decode the sum we will get our final answer.

So,

Code for 14th - 0 (remainder obtained by dividing 14 with 7)

Code for March- 4

Code for 2020- 3 (since the month is March)

By adding 0, 4, and 3, we get

0+4+3=7

Since we know that 7 stands for the 7th day of the week and the 7th day of the week is Saturday.

Therefore, the day on 14th March 2020 was Saturday.

Hence solved.

Example 2: What was the day on 16th April 2020?

Solution 2: To find the day on 16th April 2020, we will:

S1- Encode the date, month, and year.

S2- Add all three encodes.

S3- Decode the sum we got to get our final answer.

So,

Code for 16th- 2 (remainder obtained by dividing 16 with 7)

Code for April- 0

Code for 2020- 3 (Since the month is April)

By adding 2, 0, and 3, we get

2+0+3=5

Remainder when 5 is divided by 7 is 5. We know that 5 is linked to Thursday.

Therefore, the day on 16th April 2020 was Thursday.

Hence solved.

Example 3: What was the day on 2nd October 2020?

Solution 3: To find the day on 2nd October 2020, we will:

S1- Encode the date, month, and year.

S2- Add all three encodes.

S3- Decode the sum we got to get our final answer.

So,

Code for 2nd- 2 (remainder obtained by dividing 2 with 7)

Code for October- 1

Code for 2020- 3 (Since the month is October)

By adding 2, 1, and 3, we get

2+1+3=6

Remainder when 6 is divided by 7 is 6. We know that 6 is linked to Friday.

Therefore, the day on 2nd October 2020 was Friday.

Hence solved.

Q1. Which day was on:

1)   9th March 2020

2)   13th November 2020

3)   27th October 2020

4)   18th March 2020

5)   19th June 2020

2001 to 2005 Years Calendar

Codes for each year are given below. The rest of the process and codes for dates and months will remain the same.

Year	Code(s)
2001	0
2002	1
2003	2
2004 (Leap year)	Jan & Feb-3 Mar to Dec- 4
2005	5

Table 5.3- 2001-2005 codes

Example 4: What was the day on 3rd April 2001?

Solution 4: To find the day on 3rd April 2001, we will:

S1- Encode the date, month, and year.

S2- Add all three encodes.

S3- Decode the sum we got to get our final answer.

So,

Code for 3rd- 3 (remainder obtained by dividing 3 with 7)

Code for April- 0

Code for 2001 - 0

By adding 3, 0, and 0, we get

3+0+0=3

Remainder when 3 is divided by 7 is 3. We know that 3 is linked to Tuesday.

Therefore, the day on 3rd April 2001 was Tuesday.

Hence solved.

S1- Encode the date, month, and year.

S2- Add all three encodes.

S3- Decode the sum we got to get our final answer.

So,

Code for 26th- 5 (remainder obtained by dividing 26 with 7)

Code for March- 4

Code for 2004- 4 (since the month is March)

By adding 5, 4, and 4, we get

5+4+4=13

Remainder when 13 is divided by 7 is 6. We know that 6 is linked to Friday.

Therefore, the day on 26th March 2004 was Friday.

Hence solved.

Exercise 5.2

Q1.Which day was on:

1)   18th March 2001

2)   1st September 2002

3)   7th December 2003

4)   29th March 2004

5)   2nd August 2005

2006 to 2010 Years Calendar

Codes for each year are given below. The rest of the process and codes for dates and months will remain the same.

Years	Code(s)
2006	-1
2007	0
2008	Jan & Feb- 1
(Leap year)	Mar to Dec- 2
2009	3
2010	4

Table 5.3- 2006-2010 codes

Example 6: **What was the day on 5th March 2006?**

Solution 6: **To find the day on 5th March 2006, we will:**

S1- Encode the date, month, and year.

S2- Add all three encodes.

S3- Decode the sum we will get our final answer.

So,

Code for 5th- 5 (remainder obtained by dividing 5 with 7)

Code for March- 4

Code for 2006- (-)1

> **Note:** Here, we will not add -1 with other codes. We will use this -1 later.

By adding 5 and 4, we get

5+4=9

Remainder when 9 is divided by 7 is 2. We know that 2 is linked to Monday. Here, we will need to subtract one day as the code for 2006 was -1.

Therefore, the day on 5th March 2006 was Sunday.

Hence solved.

Example 7: **What was the day on 19th May 2008?**

Solution 7: **To find the day on 19th May 2008, we will:**

S1- Encode the date, month, and year.

S2- Add all three encodes.

S3- Decode the sum we will get our final answer.

So,

Code for 19th- 5 (remainder obtained by dividing 19 with 7)

Code for May- 2

Code for 2008- 2 (since the month is May)

By adding 5, 2, and 2, we get

5+2+2=9

Remainder when 9 is divided by 7 is 2. We know that 2 is linked to Monday.

Therefore, the day on 19th May 2008 was Monday.

Hence solved.

Exercise 5.3

Q1. Which day was on:

1)   9th May 2006

2)   12th April 2007

3)   20th January 2008

4)   9th February 2009

5)   10th August 2010

2011 to 2019 Years Calendar

Codes for each year are given below. The rest of the process and codes for dates and months will remain the same.

Years	Code(s)
Year	Code(s)
2011	5
2012	Jan & Feb- 0
(Leap year)	Mar to Dec-1
2013	1
2014	2
2015	3
2016	Jan & Feb- 4
(Leap year)	Mar to Dec- 5
2017	-1
2018	0
2019	1

Table 5.3- 2011-2019 codes

Example 8: **What was the day on 16th February 2016?**

Solution 8: **To find the day on 16th February 2016, we will:**

S1- Encode the date, month, and year.

S2- Add all three encodes.

S3- Decode the sum we got to get our final answer.

So,

Code for 16th- 2 (remainder obtained by dividing 16 with 7)

Code for February- 4

Code for 2016- 4 (since the month is February)

By adding 2, 4, and 4, we get

2+4+4=10

Remainder when 10 is divided by 7 is 3. We know that 3 is linked to Tuesday.

Therefore, the day on 16th February 2016 was Tuesday.

Hence solved.

Example 9: **What was the day on 9th July 2017?**

Solution 9: **To find the day on 9th July 2017, we will:**

S1- Encode the date, month, and year.

S2- Add all three encodes.

S3- Decode the sum we got to get our final answer.

So,

Code for 9th- 2 (remainder obtained by dividing 9 with 7)

Code for July- 0

Code for 2017- (-)1

Note: Here, we will not add -1 with other codes. We will use this -1 later.

By adding 2 and 0, we get

2+0=2

Remainder when 2 is divided by 7 is 2. We know that 2 is linked to Monday. Here, we will need to subtract one day as the code for 2017 was -1.

Therefore, the day on 9th July 2017 was Sunday.

Hence solved.

 *Exercise 5.4*

Q1. Which day was on:

1) 8th March 2011

2) 29th August 2013

3) 16th May 2018

4) 19th July 2012

5) 7th January 2016

WORKSHEET-6

1) **Which day was on 30th July 2020?**
   a) Monday b) Thursday c) Tuesday

2) **Which day was on 8th Nov 2020?**
   a) Sunday b) Wednesday c) Monday

3) **Which day was on 21st May 2008?**
   a) Monday b) Tuesday c) Wednesday

4) **Which day was on 5th Jan 2014?**
   a) Sunday b) Thursday c) Friday

5) **Which day was on 10th Sept 2001?**
   a) Monday b) Tuesday c) Saturday

6) **Which day was on 10th Sept 2007?**
   a) Monday b) Tuesday c) Saturday

7) **Which day was on 20th July 2006?**
   a) Monday b) Sunday c) Tuesday

8) **Which day was on 7th April 2009?**
   a) Sunday b) Monday c) Saturday

9) **Which day was on 18th Dec 2004?**
   a) Friday b) Thursday c) Saturday

10) **Which day was on 3rd July 2003?**
   a) Tuesday b) Thursday c) Monday

Magical Calendar Part-2

1900 to 1999 Years Calendar

Now, we will learn the easiest and most effective way to calculate the day of any date between 1900 to 1999. In this way, we will be able to master the days of 100 years. This seems impossible if we try without using shortcut techniques, but with Vedic maths, it will become a cakewalk.

Calculate Year Codes Comfortably

To calculate the year code, we will first divide the year into two halves: the century code and the year code. The first two digits of the year are a part of the century code, and the last two digits are a part of the year code. The century code will remain the same for the entire span of 100 years (1900 to 1999), whereas the year code may differ with each year. We will have to remember that the century code for the 20th century (1900 to 1999) is 0.

Now, to calculate the year code, we will apply a new formula, QAR4+7. Here, Q stands for quotient, A for addition, and R for remainder. In this rule, we will first divide the year with 4, then add its quotient to the year and further divide the sum by 7. The remainder obtained will be the year code.

Quotient obtained by dividing the year by 4.	Addition of the year and the quotient.	Remainder obtained by dividing the sum by 7.
Q/4	Y+Q/4	(Y+Q/4)/7

Q | A | R

4 | + | 7

We can learn the QAR4+7 formula using memory tricks. QAR can be remembered by thinking of a car, and 4 and 7 can be considered as the car's 4 wheels and 7 seats. Let's apply this formula in some questions.

Example 10: **Find the year code for 1916.**

(To find the year code, we:

Step 1- Use the QAR4+7

Q | A | R

4 | + | 7 formula and divide the last two digits by 4 to get Q.

Step 2- Add Q to the year [last two digits].

Step 3- Divide the answer by 7.)

S1- Divide 16 by 4 and write it properly.

16/4=4 (Q)

4|16|

S2- Add Q to the year (16) and write it properly.

16+4=20

4|16|

  +4

  20

S3- Divide the answer by 7.

When 20 is divided by 7, the quotient will be 2, and the remainder will be 6.

4|16|

  +4

7|20|2

   14

    6

Therefore, the year code is 6. And we know that the century code for 19 is 0. So, the code for 1916 is 06.

Hence solved.

Example 11:   **Find the year code for 1922.**

Solution 11:   **To get the year code, we will:**

S1- Divide 22 by 4 and write it properly.

22/4=5 (approx.)

5|22|

S2- Add Q to the year (22) and write it properly.

22+5=27

5|22|

  +5

  27

S3- Divide the answer by 7.

When 27 is divided by 7, the quotient will be 3, and the remainder will be 6.

  5|22|

   +5

  7|27|3

     21

      6

Therefore, the year code is 6. And we know that the century code for 19 is 0. So, the code for 1922 is 06.

Hence solved.

Example 12: Find the year code for 1944.

Solution 12: To get the year code, we will:

S1- Divide 44 by 4 and write it properly.

44/4=11

11|44|

S2- Add Q to the year (44) and write it properly.

44+11=55

11|44|

  +11

   55

S3- Divide the answer by 7.

When 44 is divided by 7, the quotient will be 7, and the remainder will be 6.

11|44|

  +11

 7|55|7

   49

      6

Therefore, the year code is 6. And we know that the century code for 19 is 0. So, the code for 1944 is 06.

Hence solved.

Exercise 5.5

Q1. Find year codes of the following.

1.　　1918
2.　　1923
3.　　1955
4.　　1978
5.　　1998

Therefore, the y

Find the Exact Day

After finding the year code using the QAR4+7 formula, we will find the exact day by adding the date, day, century, and year codes together. The sum obtained will be the final answer.

If the sum obtained is greater than 7, we will further subtract it from 7.

Let us look at some examples to understand the topic further.

S1- Find the codes for the given date and month.

The remainder obtained by dividing the date by 7 will be the date's code.

The code for the date is 19/7=5.

The code for May is 2.

S2- Find the code for the given year (1902).

The century code for 19 is 0.

We will find the year code for 02 using QAR4+7. So, divide 02 by 4 but as 02 is smaller than 4, therefore the code will be considered as 2.

Therefore, the code for 1902 is 02.

S3- Find the final code by adding all codes.

5+2+0+2=9

=9-7 (as date should be less than 7)

=2

We know that 2 is the code for Monday.

Therefore, the day was Monday.

Hence solved.

Example 14: **What was the day on 26 July 1904?**

Solution 14: **To find the date, we will:**

S1- Find the codes for the given date and month.

The code for the date is the remainder of 26/7, i.e., 5.

The code for July is 0.

S2- Find the code for the given year (1904).

The century code for 19 is 0.

We will find the year code for 02 using QAR4+7.

1.   1|04|

2.   1|04|

            +1

              5

3.   As 5 is not divisible by 7, therefore 5 will be considered as the year code.

S3- Find the final code by adding all codes.

5+0+0+5=10

=10-7

=3

We know that 3 is the code for Tuesday.

Therefore, the day was Tuesday.

Hence solved.

Example 15: What was the day on 16 June 1912?

Solution 15: To find the date, we will:

S1- Find the codes for the given date and month.

The code for the date is the remainder of 16/7, i.e., 2.

The code for June is 5.

S2- Find the code for the given year (1912).

The century code for 19 is 0.

We will find the year code for 02 using QAR4+7.

1.   3|12|

2.   3|12
       +3
       15

3.   3|12|
       +3
    7|15|2
       14
        1

Therefore, the code for 1912 is 01.

S3- Find the final code by adding all codes.

     2+5+0+1=8

=8-7

=1

We know that 1 is the code for Sunday.

Therefore, the day was Sunday.

Hence solved.

Example 16: What was the day on 7 September 1922?

Solution 16: To find the date, we will:

S1- Find the codes for the given date and month.

The code for the date is the remainder of 7/7, i.e., 0.

The code for September is 6.

S2- Find the code for the given year (1922).

The century code for 19 is 0.

We will find the year code for 22 using QAR4+7.

1.   5|22|

2.   5|22
       +5
       27

3.   5|22|

        +5

     7|27|3

        21

         6

Therefore, the code for 1922 is 06.

S3- Find the final code by adding all codes.

0+6+0+6=12

=12-7

=5

We know that 5 is the code for Thursday.

Therefore, the day was Thursday.

Hence solved.

 What was the day on 18 September 1934?

 To find the date, we will:

S1- Find the codes for the given date and month.

The code for date is remainder of 18/7, i.e., 4.

The code for September is 6.

S2- Find the code for the given year (1934).

The century code for 19 is 0.

We will find the year code for 34 using QAR4+7.

1.   8|34|

2.   8|34

          +8

          42

3.   8|34

          +8

     7|42|6

          42

           0

Therefore, the code for 1922 is 06.

S3- Find the final code by adding all codes.

4+6+0+0=10

=10-7

=3

We know that 3 is the code for Tuesday.

Therefore, the day was Tuesday.

Hence solved.

Q1. What was the day on the following dates?

1)   18 January 1919

2)   22 March 1992

3)   16 May 1909

4)   7 July 1999

5)   27 October 1954

WORKSHEET-7

100 Years Calendar (1900-1999)

Find the days of the following dates :

1) 2 Jan 1903 =	2) 21 June 1952 =
3) 14 Dec 1909 =	4) 19 Nov 1963 =
5) 9 Feb 1912 =	6) 24 March 1944 =
7) 18 Sep 1918 =	8) 3 April 1936 =
9) 5 July 1915 =	10) 5 Oct 1942 =
11) 2 Nov 1926 =	12) 16 Dec 1956 =
13) 6 May 1929 =	14) 19 Feb 1964 =
15) 9 Oct 1942 =	16) 3 May 1932 =
17) 26 April 1919 =	18) 17 March 1932 =
19) 15 Nov 1945 =	20) 26 June 1986 =

5c Magical Calendar Part-3

2000 to 2099 Years Calendar

Here, we will learn the trick to calculate the day of any date between 2000 to 2099 comfortably. By learning this trick, we will be able to solve every question related to the calendar in exams.

I have made a world record by preparing an unlimited years calendar, and this trick has been extremely useful to me in achieving this feat.

The calculation process of the day will remain completely same as in the last case, but the code for the century year (20) for 2000-2099 will be 6. Let's look at some examples to understand better.

Example 18: What was the day on 17 November 2023?

Solution 18: To find the date, we will:

S1- Find the codes for the given date and month.

The code for the date is the remainder of 17/7, i.e., 3.

The code for November is 4.

S2- Find the code for the given year (2023).

The century code for 20 is 6.

We will find the year code for 23 using QAR4+7.

1.   5|23|

2.   5|23|

        +5

        28

3.   5|23|

        +5

     7|28|4

        28

        0

Therefore, the code for 2023 is 60.

S3- Find the final code by adding all codes.

3+4+6+0

=13-7

=6

We know that 6 is the code for Friday.

Therefore, the day will be Friday.

Hence solved.

Example 19: **What will be the day on 1 December 2029?**

Solution 19: **To find the date, we will:**

S1- Find the codes for the given date and month.

The code for the date, 1 is 1, as it is not divisible by 7.

The code for December is 6.

S2- Find the code for the given year (2029).

The century code for 20 is 6.

We will find the year code for 29 using QAR4+7.

1. 7|29|

2. 7|29|

    +7

    36

3. 7|29|

    +7

    7|36|5

    35

    1

Therefore, the code for 2029 is 61.

S3- Find the final code by adding all codes.

1+6+6+1

=14-7

=7

We know that 7 is the code for Saturday.

Therefore, the day will be Saturday.

Hence solved.

Example 20: **What will be the day on 16 November 2036?**

Solution 20: **To find the date, we will:**

S1- Find the codes for the given date and month.

The code for the date is the remainder of 16/7, i.e., 2.

The code for November is 4.

S2- Find the code for the given year (2036).

The century code for 20 is 6.

We will find the year code for 36 using QAR4+7.

1. 9|36|

2.   9|36|

        +9

        45

3.   9|36|

        +9

        7|45|6

        42

        3

Therefore, the code for 2036 is 63.

S3- Find the final code by adding all codes.

2+4+6+3

=15-7

=1

We know that 1 is the code for Sunday.

Therefore, the day will be Sunday.

Hence solved.

 What will be the day on 1 March 2044?

 To find the date, we will:

S1- Find the codes for the given date and month.

The code for the date, 1 is 1 as it is not divisible by 7.

The code for March is 4.

S2- Find the code for the given year (2044).

The century code for 20 is 6.

We will find the year code for 44 using QAR4+7.

1.   11|44|

2.   11|44|

        +11

        55

3.   11|44|

        +11

        7|55|7

        49

        6

Therefore, the code for 2044 is 66.

S3- Find the final code by adding all codes.

1+4+6+6

=17-7

=10-7

=3

We know that 3 is the code for Tuesday.

Therefore, the day will be Tuesday.

Hence solved.

 What will be the day on 19 June 2062?

 To find the date, we will:

S1- Find the codes for the given date and month.

The code for the date is 5.

The code for the month is 5.

S2- Find the code for the given year.

The century code for 20 is 6.

We will find the year code for 62 using QAR4+7, which will be 0.

Therefore, the code for 2062 is 60.

S3- Find the final code by adding all codes.

5+5+6+0

=16-7

=9-7

=2

We know that 2 is the code for Monday.

Therefore, the day will be Monday.

Hence solved.

 What will be the day on 1 October 2069?

 To find the date, we will:

S1- Find the codes for the given date and month.

The code for the date is 1.

The code for the month is 1.

S2- Find the code for the given year.

The century code for 20 is 6.

We will find the year code for 69 using QAR4+7, which will be 2.

Therefore, the code for 2069 is 62.

S3- Find the final code by adding all codes.

1+1+6+2

=10-7=3

We know that 3 is the code for Tuesday.

Therefore, the day will be Tuesday.

Hence solved.

S1- Find the codes for the given date and month.

The code for the date is 2.

The code for the month is 0.

S2- Find the code for the given year.

The century code for 20 is 6.

We will find the year code for 23 using QAR4+7, which will be 0.

Therefore, the code for 2023 is 60.

S3- Find the final code by adding all codes.

2+0+6+0

=8-7=1

We know that 1 is the code for Sunday.

Therefore, the day will be Sunday.

Hence solved.

Example 25: What will be the day on 29 June 2075?
Solution 25: To find the date, we will:

S1- Find the codes for the given date and month.

The code for the date is 1.

The code for the month is 5.

S2- Find the code for the given year.

The century code for 20 is 6.

We will find the year code for 75 using QAR4+7, which will be 2.

Therefore, the code for 2075 is 62.

S3- Find the final code by adding all codes.

1+5+6+2

=14-7=7

We know that 7 is the code for Saturday.

Therefore, the day will be Saturday.

Hence solved.

Example 26: What will be the day on 1 February 2084?
Solution 26: To find the date, we will:

S1- Find the codes for the given date and month.

The code for the date is 1.

The code for the month is 4.

S2- Find the code for the given year.

The century code for 20 is 6.

We will find the year code for 84 using QAR4+7, which will be 0.

Therefore, the code for 2075 is 62.

S3- Find the final code by adding all codes.

1+4+6+0

=11-7=4

We know that 4 is the code for Wednesday. But as the given year is a leap year (as it is divisible by 4), so the original day will be one less than the received day, i.e., Tuesday.

Therefore, the day will be Tuesday.

Hence solved.

Exercise 5.7

Q1. What was the day on the following dates?

1)   18 January 1919

2)   22 March 1992

3)   16 May 1909

4)   7 July 1999

5)   27 October 1954

WORKSHEET-8

Find the days of the following dates :

1)	1 March 2025 =		2)	3 March 2022 =
3)	19 Jan 2033 =		4)	14 Feb 2032 =
5)	25 June 2033 =		6)	31 Dec 2044 =
7)	15 Aug 2046 =		8)	19 April 2059 =
9)	17 Sept 2048 =		10)	15 Oct 2045 =
11)	26 July 2064 =		12)	12 Nov 2042 =
13)	29 Dec 2066 =		14)	17 Dec 2023 =
15)	30 Aug 2022 =		16)	10 Nov 2034 =
17)	5 April 2044 =		18)	28 June 2054 =
19)	16 May 2049 =		20)	19 Aug 2042 =

Vedic Maths

Addition

Chapter 6

About the Chapter

This chapter is about a basic operation which, when comes in large quantity, causes fear in students. That basic operation is addition.

The chapter begins with the basic definition and knowledge of addition. The magical dot formula is discussed to increase addition speed significantly.

The theory is complemented with examples along with their detailed step-by-step solutions. Exercise and worksheet are also provided to help students in practicing and sharpening the dot method.

Addition

The addition is one of the four basic operations of arithmetic. When two or more whole numbers are put together, their output or the result is called sum. This process altogether is called addition.

By using the technique that I will be sharing, I can add many digit numbers very easily. My students have astonished the world and made world records on additions. I believe you can do it too with this secret technique.

Add Whole Numbers Quickly

To add whole numbers faster, we will apply the dot method. This is a new yet easy method to solve questions related to addition.

In the dot method, we will add all the digits belonging to the same place of the given numbers and put a dot wherever the sum becomes equal to or more than 10. After a dot is applied to the LHS of the digit, whatever is left after taking out 10 from the digits will be considered and added further. All the dots of place of the digits will be added together, and their sum will be added to the first digit of the next place and so on...

Don't worry, you will be able to completely understand what is being discussed here by referring to the examples given below. (Example 1 provides the most detailed solution by explaining every step in detail.)

Note: This trick may take time initially, but with practice it can be completed within seconds.

(To find the sum of numbers, we will:

Step 1- Add the ones place digits together.

Step 2- Add the number of dots to the first digit of the tens place and find the sum of all tens place digits.

Step 3- Add the number of dots to the first digit of the hundreds place and find the sum of all hundreds place digits.

Step 4- Add the number of dots to the first digit of the thousands place and find the sum of all thousands place digits.)

Solution 1: To add these numbers, we will:

S1- Add the ones digits together.

8+4=12, which is more than 10.

Therefore, put a dot before 4 to show that the sum is more than 10. As 2 is left out (12-10), add 2 to the next digit, which is 8.

8+2=10

Put a dot before 8 to indicate that the sum is 10. Then, we are left with the last digit of unit place, which is 8.

Therefore, after adding ones place digits, we get the answer as 8 and two dots.

```
  6 3 4 8
  5 6 7.4
  9 2 6.8
+ 9 5 4 8
----------------
          8
----------------
```

S2- Add the number of dots to the first digit of the next place (tens place).

As there are two dots, add 2 to 4.

2+4=6

Add 6 to the next digit, which is 7.

6+7=13, which is more than 10.

Therefore, put a dot before 7. As 3 is left out (13-10), add it to the next digit, 6.

3+6=9

As it is less than 10, therefore, directly add it to the last digit, 4.

9+4=13

Put a dot on 4 as the sum is more than 10. Therefore, the sum of tens digit will be 3 (13-10).

```
  6 3 4 8
  5 6.7.4
  9 2 6.8
+ 9 5.4 8
----------------
        3 8
----------------
```

S3- Add the number of dots to the first digit of hundreds place. Then add the rest of the numbers.

As there are two dots, we will add 2 to 3.

2+3=5

Add 5 to the next digit, which is 6.

5+6=11, which is more than 10.

Therefore, put a dot before 6. As 1 is left out (11-10), add it to the next digit, 2.

1+2=3

As it is less than 10, therefore directly add it to the last digit, 5.

3+5=8

Therefore, the sum of hundreds digit will be 8.

```
  6 3 4 8
  5.6.7.4
  9 2 6.8
+ 9 5.4 8
-----------
    8 3 8
```

S4- Add the number of dots to the first digit of thousands place. Then add rest of the numbers.

As there is one dots, add 1 to 6.

1+6=7

Add 7 to the next digit, which is 5.

7+5=12, which is more than 10.

Therefore, put a dot before 5. As 2 is left out (12-10), add it to the next digit, 9.

2+9=11

Put a dot before 9 to show that the sum is more than 10. As 1 is left out (11-10), add 1 to the next digit, which is 9.

1+9=10

As the sum is equal to 10, put a dot before 9. Therefore, the sum of thousands digit will be 0.

```
   6 3 4 8
  .5.6.7.4
  .9 2 6.8
+ .9 5.4 8
-----------
   0 8 3 8
```

As we have 3 dots on the thousands place, therefore, we will put 3 before 0.

So, the final answer is 30838.

Hence solved.

Solution 2:   To add these numbers, we will:

S1- Add the unit digits together.

4+8=12

Put a dot before 8, add 2 to the next digit, 4.

2+4=6

Add 6 to last digit, 5.

6+5=11

Put a dot before 5. The final sum of all ones place digits is 1.

S2- Add the number of dots to the first digit of the next place (tens place). Then, add all digits.

As there are two dots, add 2 to 5.

2+5=7

Add 7 to the next digit, 9.

7+9=16

Put dot on 9, add 6 to 5.

6+5=11

Put dot on 5, add 1 to last digit 6.

1+6=7

The final sum of all tens place digits is 7.

```
  7 6 5 4
  3 8.9.8
  6 7.5 4
+ 3 9 6 5
-------------
      7 1
```

S3- Add the number of dots to the first digit of the next place (hundreds place). Then, add all digits.

As there are two dots, add 2 to 6.

2+6=8

Add 8 to the next digit, 8.

8+8=16

Put a dot on 8 and add 6 to the next digit, 7.

6+7=13

Put a dot on 7 and add 3 to the last digit, 9.

3+9=12

The final sum of all hundreds place digits is 2.

S4- Add the number of dots to the first digit of the next place (thousands place). Then, add all digits.

As there are three dots, add 3 to the first digit, 7.

3+7=10

Put a dot on 7 and add next digit, 3 to its next digit, 6.

3+6=9

Add 9 to the next digit, 3

9+3=12

Put a dot on 3. The final sum of thousands place digits is 2.

As we are left with two dots in the thousands place, therefore, we will put 2 before 2.

```
 .7 6 5 4
 3.8.9.8
 6.7.5 4
+.3.9 6.5
2 2 2 7 1
```

So, the final answer is 22271.

Hence solved.

Exercise 6.1

Q1. Add the given numbers together.

1)   86745, 98965, 43674, 28965
2)   3248, 6556, 7493, 8674, 3258
3)   6457, 7896, 4365, 5493, 7578
4)   67582, 93864, 28773, 36784, 42389
5)   765482, 986754, 367897, 435968, 224379

Example 3:	**Add 67582, 93864, 28773, 36784, 42389.**
Solution 3:	To add these numbers, we will:

S1- Add the unit digits together.

1)   Add 2+4=6
2)   Add 6+3=9
3)   Add 2+4=6
4)   Add 6+3=9
5)   Add 9+4=13
6)   Since 13>10, therefore, put a dot before 4 and add the remaining value, i.e., 3 with 9. So, 3+9=12
7)   In the answer box write 2.

8) Now add the dots (2 in this case) and add them to the first digit of the next place digit row.

S2- Repeat the same steps of addition for the rest of the sum until the ten thousandth place.

S3- Finally, add the dots remaining on the LHS of ten thousandth row and note down their sum.

So,

67582
+93864
+28773
+36784
+42389
269392

Therefore, the sum of the given numbers is 269392.

Hence solved.

WORKSHEET-9

Q1. Solve the following sums.

1)	2 3 5 4	2)	6 7 2 4	3)	3 7 3 2
	4 3 6 2		5 4 8 1		4 5 4 8
+	7 4 3 6	+	3 3 9 2	+	9 1 2 3
	2 5 8 1		2 0 5 4		6 6 4 5

4)	7 6 5 4	5)	9 2 1 3	6)	7 6 6 2
	8 1 9 2		3 6 4 4		4 3 5 4
+	2 8 4 4	+	7 2 5 4	+	8 1 9 3
	3 3 6 2		8 1 9 3		3 0 7 6

Vedic Maths

7) 4 3 5 6
    7 8 9 1
+   3 6 4 5
    8 1 2 4
    _ _ _ _ _ _ _ _
    _ _ _ _ _ _ _ _

8) 3 6 4 2
    5 4 7 8
    9 1 2 3
    3 7 4 5
    _ _ _ _ _ _ _
    _ _ _ _ _ _ _

9) 3 4 5 4 2
    6 7 8 9 3
    2 1 4 5 3
    7 7 6 2 4
    _ _ _ _ _ _ _ _
    _ _ _ _ _ _ _ _

10) 5 4 8 1 2
    3 4 6 1 3
+   2 1 4 5 3
    7 7 6 2 4
    _ _ _ _ _ _ _ _
    _ _ _ _ _ _ _ _

11) 7 8 5 4 2
    8 9 6 5 4
+   7 0 2 1 4
    8 1 1 5 6
    _ _ _ _ _ _ _
    _ _ _ _ _ _ _

12) 5 9 8 1 2
    3 6 7 8 4
+   4 5 9 4 6
    7 8 1 3 7
    _ _ _ _ _ _ _ _
    _ _ _ _ _ _ _ _

13) 3 4 5 2 3
    9 1 2 7 6
+   3 8 4 2 4
    1 3 6 7 2
    _ _ _ _ _ _ _ _
    _ _ _ _ _ _ _ _

14) 7 6 5 4 2
    3 9 4 8 1
+   3 7 2 4 5
    8 1 9 1 2
    _ _ _ _ _ _ _
    _ _ _ _ _ _ _

15) 8 2 4 3 2
    6 7 5 8 1
+   9 9 4 7 4
    3 6 5 8 1
    _ _ _ _ _ _ _
    _ _ _ _ _ _ _

16) 9 8 9 7 2
    6 7 4 2 5
+   8 1 3 6 4
    3 4 6 8 1
    _ _ _ _ _ _ _
    _ _ _ _ _ _ _

17) 9 9 5 4 3
    8 1 9 6 7
+   4 5 2 8 2
    2 4 3 4 8
    _ _ _ _ _ _ _
    _ _ _ _ _ _ _

18) 4 3 5 4 6
    7 8 9 9 8
+   3 6 4 5 2
    7 6 9 1 4
    _ _ _ _ _ _ _
    _ _ _ _ _ _ _

19) 9 7 3 2 4
    8 1 6 5 8
+   3 3 4 2 5
    7 6 9 1 4
    _ _ _ _ _ _ _ _
    _ _ _ _ _ _ _ _

20) 4 5 5 4 3
    8 1 9 2 6
+   7 7 6 5 4
    8 1 9 3 6
    _ _ _ _ _ _ _
    _ _ _ _ _ _ _

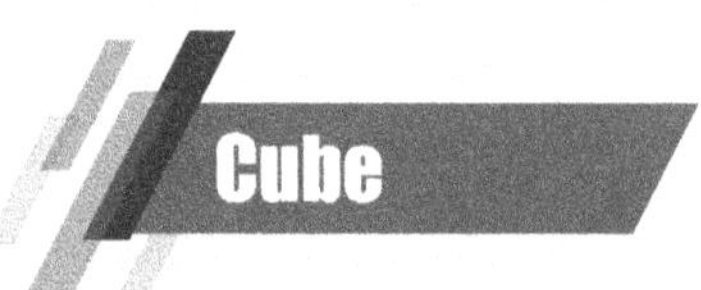

About the Chapter

This chapter is devoted to the study of a useful and common concept of cubes.

It begins with the basic definition and knowledge of cubes. For ease of understanding, cubes are divided into two parts: general and specific.

It contains solved examples and exercises in sufficient quantity. Also, the chapter provides worksheets of various difficulty levels to make the learning process interesting and practical.

Cube

Cube is the product of a number which is obtained by multiplying the same number by itself thrice. For example, the cube of 2 is 23=2x2x2=8.

Like all the other topics, cubes are also divided into two types:

1. Specific cubes
2. General cubes

Specific Cubes

Specific cubes are the cube techniques that are limited to certain specific numbers or situations. These techniques are direct and don't include a pen or paper most of the time.

This is further divided into two categories:

1) Above the base number
2) Below the base number

Above the Base Number

Every number in mathematics has its base number, as we already know. The technique that we will study here will require the concept of the near base. The numbers which exceed their near base falls under this category. For example, 106 exceeds its near base 100 by 6 digits.

To find the cube of "above the base numbers," we will first divide our answer into three parts, i.e., LHS/Middle/RHS. We will find the surplus of the number from its near base and then calculate the LHS. To calculate the LHS, we will first double the surplus and then add it to the given number and note it in the answer box. Then we will find out the middle part; for that, we will square the surplus and then multiply the product with three (3) and then note the final product in the answer box. For RHS, we will find the cube of the surplus and write it in the answer box.

With this technique, you will be able to effortlessly calculate cubes from 101 to 120, 1001 to 1020, 10001 to 10020, etc.

> **Note:** The middle part and the RHS should be balanced with the base. In case it is not balanced, we shall use the carry forward method or balance it using zero(es).

Example 1: **Find the cube of 102.**

(To find the cube, we:

Step 1- Find the surplus from the nearest base.

Step 2- Double the surplus and add it to the number to get the LHS.

Step 3- Find the square of surplus and multiply it by 3 to get the middle part (M).

Step 4- Find the cube of surplus to get the RHS.

Step 5- Combine LHS, M, and RHS and balance the number according to base.)

Solution 1: To find the cube of 102, we will:

S1- Calculate the surplus of the given number from its nearest base.

Here, 2 is the surplus (102-100).

S2- Double the surplus and add it to the number to get the LHS.

$2 \times 2 = 4$; $4 + 102 = 106$ (this will be our LHS)

S3- Find the square of surplus and multiply it by 3 to get the M.

$2^2 = 4$; $4 \times 3 = 12$ (this will be our M)

S4- Find the cube of surplus to get the RHS.

$2^3 = 8$ (this will be our RHS)

S5- Combine LHS, M, and RHS and balance the number according to base.

LHS/M/RHS

106/12/08

We have put 0 before 8 to balance the base of 8 with the base 100.

Therefore, $102^3 = 1061208$

Hence solved.

Example 2: Find the cube of 104.

Solution 2: To find the cube of 104, we will:

S1- Calculate the surplus of the given number from its nearest base.

Here, 4 is the surplus (104-100).

S2- Double the surplus and add it to the number to get the LHS.

$4 \times 2 = 8$; $8 + 104 = 112$ (this will be our LHS)

S3- Find the square of surplus and multiply it by 3 to get the M.

$4^2 = 16$; $16 \times 3 = 48$ (this will be our M)

S4- Find the cube of surplus to get the RHS.

4^3=64 (this will be our RHS)

S5- Combine LHS, M, and RHS and balance the number according to base.

LHS/M/RHS

112/48/64

All the numbers are already balanced.

Therefore, 1043= 1124864

Hence solved.

Example 3: **Find the cube of 1002.**

Solution 3: To find the cube of 1002, we will:

S1- Calculate the surplus of the given number from its nearest base.

Here, 2 is the surplus (1002-1000).

S2- Double the surplus and add it to the number to get the LHS.

2x2=4; 4+1002=1006 (this will be our LHS)

S3- Find the square of surplus and multiply it by 3 to get the M.

2^2=4; 4x3=12 (this will be our M)

S4- Find the cube of surplus to get the RHS.

2^3=8 (this will be our RHS)

S5- Combine LHS, M, and RHS and balance the number according to base.

LHS/M/RHS

1006/012/008

We have put 0s before 12 and 8 to balance them with the base 1000.

Therefore, 10023= 1006012008

Hence solved.

 *Exercise 7.1*

Q1. Find the cubes of the following.

1) 107^3
2) 101^3
3) 109^3
4) 106^3
5) 104^3
6) 1003^3
7) 1005^3
8) 1008^3
9) 1009^3
10) 1011^3

Below the Base Number

The numbers that do not exceed their near base falls under this category. For example, 98 is less than its near base 100 by 2 digits.

To find the cube of "below the base numbers," we will first divide our answer into three parts, i.e., LHS/Middle/RHS. Then we will find the deficiency of the number from its near base and calculate the LHS.

To find the LHS, we will first double the deficiency and then subtract the given number and note it in the answer box. Then we will find out the middle part, for that we will square the deficiency and then multiply the product by 3 and note the final product in the answer box. For RHS, we will find the cube of the surplus and write it in the answer box with a bar (denoting a negative sign due to the classic sign rule).

To remove the bar, we will simply subtract 1 from the middle part and write the complement of the initial RHS.

> **Note:** The middle part and the RHS should be balanced with the base. In case it is not balanced, we shall use the carry forward method or balance it using zero(es) or subtraction method.

Example 4: **Find the cube of 98.**

(To obtain the cube, we will:

Step 1 - Calculate the deficiency of the given number from its actual base.

Step 2 - Double the deficiency and subtract it from the number to get the LHS.

Step 3 - Find the square of deficiency and multiply it by 3 to get the middle part (M).

Step 4 - Find the cube of deficiency and put a bar over it (as the answer will be negative). To remove the bar, subtract one from M and take the complement of cube value to get the RHS.

Step 5 - Combine LHS, M, and RHS and balance the numbers as per the base.

Solution 4: To find the cube of 98, we will:

S1 - Calculate the deficiency of the given number from its actual base.

Deficiency is 2 in this case (100-98).

S2 - Double the deficiency and subtract it from the number to get the LHS.

2x2=4; 98-4=94 (this will be our LHS)

S3- Find the square of deficiency and multiply it by 3 to get the temporary middle part (M).

2x2=4 and 4x3=12 (this will be our initial M)

S4 - Find the cube of deficiency and put a bar over it (as the answer will be negative). To remove the bar, subtract one from M and take the complement of cube value to get the RHS.

(-2)3= (-)2x2x2=-8=8

To remove the bar,

12-1=11 (this will be our final M)

Complement of 08=92 (this will be our RHS)

S5 - Combine LHS, M, and RHS and balance the numbers as per the base.

LHS/M/RHS

94/11/92

Therefore, 983= 941192.

Hence solved.

 Find the cube of 96.

 To find the cube of 96, we will:

S1- Calculate the deficiency of the given number from its actual base.

Deficiency is 4 in this case (100-96).

S2- Double the deficiency and subtract it from the number to get the LHS.

4x2=8; 96-8=88 (this will be our LHS)

S3- Find the square of deficiency and multiply it by 3 to get the temporary middle part (M).

4x4=16 and 16x3=48 (this will be our initial M)

S4- Find the cube of deficiency and put a bar over it (as the answer will be negative). To remove the bar, subtract one from M and take the complement of cube value to get the RHS.

(-4)3= (-)4x4x4=-64=(64)

To remove the bar,

48-1=47 (this will be our final M)Complement of 64 (100-64)=36 (this will be our RHS)

S5- Combine LHS, M, and RHS and balance the numbers as per the base.

LHS/M/RHS

88/47/36

Therefore, 963= 884736.

Hence solved.

 Find the cube of 998.

 To find the cube of 998, we will:

S1- Calculate the deficiency of the given number from its actual base.

Deficiency is 2 in this case (1000-998).

S2- Double the deficiency and subtract it from the number to get the LHS.

2x2=4; 998-4=994 (this will be our LHS)

S3- Find the square of deficiency and multiply it by 3 to get the temporary middle part (M).

2x2=4 and 4x3=12 (this will be our initial M)

S4- Find the cube of deficiency and put a bar over it (as the answer will be negative). To remove the bar, subtract one from M and take the complement of cube value to get the RHS.

(-2)3= (-)2x2x2=-8=8

12 and 8 will be taken as 012 and 008 to balance them with 1000 base.

To remove the bar,

012-1=011 (this will be our final M)

Complement of 008=992 (this will be our RHS)

S5- Combine LHS, M, and RHS and balance the numbers as per the base.

LHS/M/RHS

994/011/992

Therefore, 9983= 994011992.

Hence solved.

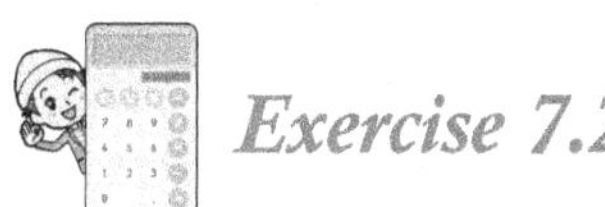

Exercise 7.2

Q1. Find the cubes of the following.

1) 92^3
2) 97^3
3) 91^3
4) 94^3
5) 998^3
6) 999^3
7) 993^3
8) 9995^3
9) 9991^3
10) 9996^3

General Cubes

General cube tricks are those which are not bound to any specific number or digits. These techniques are equally effective for all numbers. There are various categories in this.

Cubes of Two-Digit Numbers Starting with 1

This technique of cubing is applicable to two-digit numbers whose tens digit is one. This trick consists of 2 steps. Let us understand how to use this trick using examples.

Example 7:   Find the cube of 12.

(To find the cube, we:

Step 1- Write the square and the cube of ones digit towards the right of the given number.

Step 2- Write the double of hundreds digit below the hundreds digit and double of tens digit below the tens digit.

Step 3- Add Step 1 to Step 2 numbers to get the final answer.)

Solution 7:   To get the cube of 12, we will:

S1- Write the square (2^2) and the cube (2^3) of ones digit (2) towards the right of the given number (12).

1 2 4 8 (12 is the original number; 4 is the square of 2; 8 is the cube of 2)

Now, this is our number, 1248.

S2- Write the double of hundreds digit (2x2) below the hundreds digit (2) and double of tens digit (4x2) below the tens digit (4). We will not write anything below thousands and ones digit.

1 2 4 8

  4 8   (4 is the double of 2; 8 is the double of 4)

S3- Add S1 and S2 numbers.

1248

+48

1728

Therefore, the cube of 12=1728

Hence solved.

Example 8: **Find the cube of 14.**

Solution 8: To get the cube of 14, we will:

S1- Write the square (4^2) and the cube (4^3) of ones digit (4) towards the right of the given number (14).

T H T O

1 4 16 64 (14 is the original number; 16 is the square of 4; 64 is the cube of 4)

Here, we will consider thousands digit=1; hundreds digit=4; tens digit=16; ones digit=64.

S2- Write the double of hundreds digit (4x2) below the hundreds digit (4) and double of tens digit (16x2) below the tens digit (16). We will not write anything below thousands and ones digit.

1 4 16 64

  8 32   (8 is the double of 4; 32 is the double of 16)

S3- Add S1 and S2 numbers.

Start adding from RHS. The rightmost number at ones place is 64. Carry forward 6 and write 4.

1 4 16 64

+ 8 32

       4

16+32=48; 48+6=54 (6 carried forward from last part)

Write down 4 and carry forward 5.

1 4 16 64

+ 8 32

    4 4

4+8=12; 12+5=17 (5 carried forward from last part)

Write down 7 and carry forward 1.

1 4 16 64

+ 8 32

  7 4 4

1+1=2 (1 carried forward from last part)

1 4 16 64

+ 8 32

2 7 4 4

Therefore, the cube of 14=2744

Hence solved.

 *Exercise 7.3*

Q1. Find the cubes of the following.

1) 13^3
2) 15^3
3) 17^3
4) 18^3
5) 19^3

Cubes of Two-Digit Numbers Ending with 1

This trick of calculating the cube is amazing. It is applicable for two digits numbers whose tens digit is one. This trick consists of 2 steps. This technique's process is the reverse of what we studied in last case.

Example 9:   Find the cube of 21.

(To find the cube, we:

Step 1- Write the square and the cube of tens digit towards the left of the given number.

Step 2- Write the double of hundreds digit below the hundreds digit and double of tens digit below the tens digit.

Step 3- Add Step 1 to Step 2 numbers to get the final answer.)

Solution 9:   To get the cube of 21, we will:

S1- Write the square (2^2) and the cube (2^3) of tens digit (2) towards the left of the given number (21).

8 4 2 1 (8 is the cube of 2; 4 is the square of 2)

S2- Write the double of hundreds digit (4x2) below the hundreds digit (4) and double of tens digit (2x2) below the tens digit (2).

8 4 2 1

  8 4

S3- Add S1 to S2 numbers to get the final answer.

Start adding from RHS and carry forward wherever necessary.

8 4 2 1

+8 4

9 2 6 1

Therefore, the cube of 21 is 9261.

Hence solved.

Example 10:   Find the cube of 31.

Solution 10:   To get the cube of 31, we will:

S1- Write the square (3^2) and the cube (3^3) of tens digit (3) towards the left of the given number (31).

T H T O

2 7 9 3 1 (27 is the cube of 3; 9 is the square of 3)

S2- Write the double of hundreds digit (9x2) below the hundreds digit (9) and double of tens digit (3x2) below the tens digit (3).

2 7 9 3 1

   1 8 9

S3- Add S1 to S2 numbers to get the final answer.

Start adding from RHS and carry forward wherever necessary.

2 7 9 3 1

+ 1 8 9

2 9 7 9 1

Therefore, the cube of 31 is 29791.

Hence solved.

Exercise 7.4

Q1. Find the cubes of the following.

1) 41^3
2) 61^3
3) 71^3
4) 81^3
5) 91^3

Cube of Two-Digit Numbers Whose Tens and Ones Digits are the Same

In this technique, we will calculate the cube of a number whose ones digit and tens digit are the same. Let us understand the process using examples.

Example 11:   Find the cube of 11.

(To find the cube, we will:

Step 1- Write the cube of the leftmost digit four times.

Step 2- [Repeat the same steps as done in previous cases] Write the double of hundreds digit below the hundreds digit and double of tens digit below the tens digit.

Step 3- Add Step 1 and Step 2 numbers to get the final answer.)

Solution 11:   To get the cube of 11, we will:

S1- Write the cube (1^3) of the leftmost digit four times.

1 1 1 1

S2- Write the double of hundreds digit (1x2) below the hundreds digit (1) and double of tens digit (1x2) below the tens digit (1).

1 1 1 1

+2 2

S3- Add S1 and S2 numbers to get the final answer.

1 1 1 1

+2 2

1 3 3 1

Therefore, the cube of 11 is 1331.

Hence solved.

Example 12: **Find the cube of 33.**

Solution 12: To get the cube of 33, we will:

S1- Write the cube (3^3) of the leftmost digit four times.

27 27 27 27

S2- Write the double of hundreds digit (27x2) below the hundreds digit (27) and double of tens digit (27x2) below the tens digit (27).

27 27 27 27

+ 54 54

S3- Add S1 and S2 numbers to get the final answer.

27 27 27 27

+ 54 54

35 9 3 7

Therefore, the cube of 33 is 35937.

Hence solved.

Exercise 7.5

Q1. Find the cubes of the following.

1) 22^3
2) 44^3
3) 66^3
4) 88^3
5) 99^3

Cube of Random Numbers

Using certain tricks, it is easy to find out the cube of random numbers. Let us understand this process using some examples.

Example 13: **Find the cube of 23.**

(To find the cube, we will:

Step 1- Write the cube of tens and ones digits at the leftmost and rightmost ends.

Step 2- Calculate the square of tens digit and multiply it by ones digit and write it next to the leftmost digit.

Step 3- Calculate the square of ones digit and multiply it by tens digit and write it before the rightmost digit.

Step 4- [Repeat the same steps as done in previous cases] Write the double of hundreds digit below the hundreds digit and double of tens digit below the tens digit.

Step 5- Add S1 and S2 numbers to get the final answer.)

 To find the cube of 23, we will:

S1- Write the cube of tens and ones digits at the leftmost and rightmost ends.

8 _ _ 27

S2- Calculate the square of tens digit and multiply it by ones digit and write it next to the leftmost digit (2^2x3).

8 12 _ 27

S3- Calculate the square of ones digit and multiply it by tens digit and write it before the rightmost digit (3^2x2).

8 12 18 27

S4- Write the double of hundreds digit below the hundreds digit and double of tens digit below the tens digit.

8 12 18 27

   24 36

S5- Add S1 and S2 numbers to get the final answer.

8 12 18 27

+ 24 36

12 1 6 7

Therefore, the cube of 23 is 12167.

Hence solved.

 Find the cube of 32.

 To find the cube of 32, we will:

S1- Write the cube of tens and ones digits at the leftmost and rightmost ends.

27 _ _ 8

S2- Calculate the square of tens digit and multiply it by ones digit and write it next to the leftmost digit (3^2x2).

27 18 _ 8

S3- Calculate the square of ones digit and multiply it by tens digit and write it before the rightmost digit (2^2x3).

27 18 12 8

S4- Write the double of hundreds digit below the hundreds digit and double of tens digit below the tens digit.

27 18 12 8

   36 24

S5- Add S1 and S2 numbers to get the final answer.

```
27 18 12 8
+   36 24
32  7   6 8
```

Therefore, the cube of 32 is 32768.

Hence solved.

Cube of Numbers Ending with 5

This is a simple technique to calculate the cubes of numbers ending with 5 within five seconds. Let us understand this process using a few examples.

Example 15:   **Find the cube of 35.**

(To find the cube, we will:

Step 1- Find the square of the given number using previously learned square techniques.

Step 2- Multiply the square with the given number. Apply 4x2 multiplication formula of IXXXI.)

Solution 15:   To get the cube of 35, we will:

S1- Calculate the square of 35 using square finding techniques.

35x35=1225

S2- Multiply the square with 35 using the IXXXI formula.

1225x35=42875

Therefore, the cube of 35 is 42875.

Hence solved.

Example 16:   Find the cube of 45.

Solution 16:   To get the cube of 45, we will:

S1- Calculate the square of 45 using square finding techniques.

45x45=2025

S2- Multiply the square with 45 using the IXXXI formula.

2025x45=91125

Therefore, the cube of 45 is 91125.

Hence solved.

Exercise 7.6

Q1. Find the cubes of the following.

1) 25^3

2) 55^3

3) 75^3

4) 85^3

5) 95^3

Vedic Maths

Cube of Two-Digit Numbers Ending with 0

In this case, we will find the cube of a two-digit number ending with 0. Let us understand this concept using a few examples.

Example 17: Find the cube of 40.

(To find the cube, we will:

Step 1- Calculate the cube of tens digit.

Step 2- Put three 0s at the end.)

Solution 17: To get the cube of 40, we will:

S1- Calculate the cube of 4.

4x4x4=64

S2- Add three 0s after the S1 result.

64000

Therefore, the cube of 40 is 64000.

Hence solved.

Example 18: Find the cube of 60.

Solution 18: To get the cube of 60, we will:

S1- Calculate the cube of 6.

6x6x6=216

S2- Add three 0s after the S1 result.

216000

Therefore, the cube of 60 is 216000.

Hence solved.

Exercise 7.7

Q1. Find the cubes of the following.

1) 30^3

2) 50^3

3) 70^3

4) 80^3

5) 90^3

WORKSHEET-10

Cubes below the base

Q1. Find the Cubes of numbers near the base

1) 99^3 =   2) 98^3 =   3) 96^3 =

4) 97^3 =   5) 95^3 =   6) 94^3 =

7) 92^3 =   8) 93^3 =   9) 91^3 =

10) 998^3 =   11) 996^3 =   12) 999^3 =

13) 997^3 =   14) 995^3 =

Cubes above the base

Q2. Find the Cubes of numbers near the base

1) 102^3 =   2) 104^3 =   3) 101^3 =

4) 105^3 =   5) 107^3 =   6) 106^3 =

7) 108^3 =   8) 103^3 =   9) 109^3 =

10) 110^3 =   11) 1002^3 =   12) 1004^3 =

13) 1005^3 =   14) 1007^3 =   15) 1008^3 =

General Cubes

Q3. Find the Cubes of numbers

1) $12^3 =$ 2) $13^3 =$ 3) $14^3 =$

4) $15^3 =$ 5) $21^3 =$ 6) $31^3 =$

7) $41^3 =$ 8) $22^3 =$ 9) $33^3 =$

10) 32^3

Q2. Find the Cubes of numbers

1) $35^3 =$ 2) $45^3 =$ 3) $65^3 =$

4) $52^3 =$ 5) $54^3 =$ 6) $56^3 =$

7) $80^3 =$ 8) $90^3 =$ 9) $40^3 =$

Chapter 8
Square Roots

About the Chapter

This chapter is about square roots, which is a famous topic in competitive exams.

It begins with the definition and knowledge of square roots, and it contains a detailed explanation of square root calculation in simple language.

Along with the theory, the chapter contains completely solved examples with hints. It also has worksheets and exercises of various difficulty levels to help in applying the theory.

Square Roots

In mathematics, a square root of a number x is a number y such that $y^2 = x$. In other words, the square root of a number is the value of power 1/2 of that number. The square root of a number x is denoted with a "$\sqrt{}$" sign.

A number is said to be a perfect square number when it contains any of the following digits:

- 1
- 4
- 5
- 6
- 9

Quickly Calculate the Square Root of a Number

To calculate the square root of a number, first, we will segregate the number into two groups, namely the rightmost group (RHS) and leftmost group (LHS). To make the rightmost group, we will take the first two digits from right to left. Remember that our rightmost group should contain only two digits. After making the rightmost group, the rest digits will be taken in the leftmost group. The leftmost group can contain one, two, or three digits. The rest of the steps we will understand using examples.

The following table will help us while applying this technique.

 Find the square root of 4489.

(To find the square root, we will:

Step 1- Divide the number into LHS and RHS.

Step 2- Find the highest possible perfect square of LHS to solve LHS.

Step 3- Compare the rightmost digit of RHS with table 8.1 and write its corresponding ones digit of square root.

   To find the square root of 4489, we will:

S1- Divide 4489 into 44 (LHS) and 89 (RHS).

S2- Find the highest possible perfect square of 44 (LHS).

6 is the highest possible perfect square of 44. 6 will become our answer's tens digit.

S3- Compare the rightmost digit (9) of RHS with table 8.1 and write its corresponding ones digit of square root.

The corresponding ones digit of square root for 9 is 3 or 7. So, either 3 or 7 is our answer's ones digit.

Therefore, our answer can be either 63 or 67. To find the exact answer, we will take a number that lies in-between 63 and 67.

Let's take 65 and calculate its square.

To calculate square of 65, we will multiply its tens digit with tens digit+1, such that $6 \times (6+1) = 6 \times 7 = 42$ (this will be our LHS).

Then, square the ones digit $5^2 = 25$ (this will be our RHS).

Square of 65=4225.

As we can see, square of 65<given number, i.e., 4225<4489. Therefore, square of 63<given number.

So, 63 will be eliminated, and our answer will become 67.

The square root of 4489 is 67.

Hence solved.

 Find the square root of 9216.

   To find the square root of 9216, we will:

S1- Divide 9216 into 92 (LHS) and 16 (RHS).

S2- Find the highest possible perfect square of 92 (LHS).

9 is the highest possible perfect square of 92. So, 9 will become our answer's tens digit.

S3- Compare the rightmost digit (6) of RHS with table 8.1 and write its corresponding ones digit of square root.

The corresponding ones digit of square root for 6 is 4 or 6. So, either 4 or 6 is our answer's ones digit.

So, our answer can be 94 or 96. As we know, the square of 95 ($9 \times [9+1]/5 \times 5 = 9025$) is less than 9216. So, the square of 94 will be less than 9216.

Therefore, the square root of 9216 is 96.

Hence solved.

Example 3: **Find the square root of 5329.**

Solution 3: To find the square root of 5329, we will:

S1- Divide 5329 into 53 (LHS) and 29 (RHS).

S2- Find the highest possible perfect square of 53 (LHS).

7 is the highest possible perfect square of 53. So, 7 will become our answer's tens digit.

S3- Compare the rightmost digit (9) of RHS with table 8.1 and write its corresponding ones digit of square root.

The corresponding ones digit of square root for 9 is 3 or 7. So, either 3 or 7 is our answer's ones digit.

So, our answer can be 73 or 77. We will take a number that lies in between these two.

Let's take 95. As we know, the square of 75 (7x[7+1]/5x5=5625) is more than 5329. So, the square of 77 will be more than 5329.

Therefore, the square root of 5329 is 73.

Hence solved.

Example 4: **Find the square root of 3249.**

Solution 4: To find the square root of 3249, we will:

S1- Divide 3249 into 32 (LHS) and 49 (RHS).

S2- Find the highest possible perfect square of 32 (LHS).

5 is the highest possible perfect square of 32. So, 5 will become our answer's tens digit.

S3- Compare the rightmost digit (9) of RHS with table 8.1 and write its corresponding ones digit of square root.

The corresponding ones digit of square root for 9 is 3 or 7. So, either 3 or 7 is our answer's ones digit.

So, our answer can be 53 or 57. We will take a number that lies in between these two.

Let's take 55. As we know, the square of 55 (5x[5+1]/5x5=3025) is less than 3249. So, the square of 53 will be less than 3249.

Therefore, the square root of 3249 is 57.

Hence solved.

 *Exercise 8.1*

Q1. Calculate the following.

1) √4244
2) √3251
3) √5555
4) √2459
5) √9876

Solution 5:   To find the square root of 841, we will:

S1- Divide 841 into 8 (LHS) and 41 (RHS should have two-digits)

S2- Find the highest possible perfect square of 8 (LHS).

2 is the highest possible perfect square of 8. So, 2 will become our answer's tens digit.

S3- Compare the rightmost digit (1) of RHS with table 8.1 and write its corresponding ones digit of square root.

The corresponding ones digit of square root for 1 is 1 or 9. So, either 1 or 9 is our answer's ones digit.

So, our answer can be 21 or 29. We will take a number that lies in between these two.

Let's take 25. As we know, the square of 25 (2x[2+1]/5x5=625) is less than 841. So, the square of 21 will be less than 841.

Therefore, the square root of 841 is 29.

Hence solved.

Example 6:   **Find the square root of 289.**

Solution 6:   To find the square root of 289, we will:

S1- Divide 289 into 2 (LHS) and 89 (RHS should have two digits)

S2- Find the highest possible perfect square of 2 (LHS).

1 is the highest possible perfect square of 2. So, 1 will become our answer's tens digit.

S3- Compare the rightmost digit (9) of RHS with table 8.1 and write its corresponding ones digit of square root.

The corresponding ones digit of square root for 9 is 3 or 7. So, either 3 or 7 is our answer's ones digit.

So, our answer can be 13 or 17. We will take a number that lies in between these two.

Let's take 15. As we know, the square of 15 (1x[1+1]/5x5=225) is less than 289. So, the square of 13 will be less than 289.

Therefore, the square root of 289 is 17.

Hence solved.

 *Exercise 8.2*

Q1. Calculate the following.

1) $\sqrt{224}$
2) $\sqrt{345}$
3) $\sqrt{555}$
4) $\sqrt{981}$
5) $\sqrt{479}$

Example 7:   **Find the square root of 15129.**

Solution 7:   To find the square root of 15129, we will:

S1- Divide 15129 into 151 (LHS) and 29 (RHS).

S2- Find the highest possible perfect square of 151 (LHS).

12 is the highest possible perfect square of 151. So, 12 will become our answer's tens digit.

S3- Compare the rightmost digit (9) of RHS with table 8.1 and write its corresponding ones digit of square root.

The corresponding ones digit of square root for 9 is 3 or 7. So, either 3 or 7 is our answer's ones digit.

So, our answer can be 123 or 127. We will take a number that lies in between these two.

Let's take 125. As we know, the square of 125 (12x[12+1]/5x5=15625) is more than 15129. So, the square of 127 will be more than 15129.

Therefore, the square root of 15129 is 123.

Hence solved.

Example 8:   **Find the square root of 12321.**

Solution 8:   To find the square root of 12321, we will:

S1- Divide 12321 into 123 (LHS) and 21 (RHS).

S2- Find the highest possible perfect square of 123 (LHS).

11 is the highest possible perfect square of 123. So, 11 will become our answer's tens digit.

S3- Compare the rightmost digit (1) of RHS with table 8.1 and write its corresponding ones digit of square root.

The corresponding ones digit of square root for 1 is 1 or 9. So, either 1 or 9 is our answer's ones digit.

So, our answer can be 111 or 119. We will take a number that lies in between these two.

Let's take 115. As we know, the square of 115 (11x[11+1]/5x5=13225) is more than 12321. So, the square of 119 will be more than 12321.

Therefore, the square root of 12321 is 111.

Hence solved.

Exercise 8.2

Q1. Calculate the following.

1)   √17996

2)   √14544

3)   √12236

4)   √11661

5)   √10409

Square Roots at a Glance

Q1. Write the square roots of the following perfect squares

1) $\sqrt{1024}$ = 	2) $\sqrt{1156}$ = 	3) $\sqrt{1369}$ =

4) $\sqrt{1521}$ = 	5) $\sqrt{1764}$ = 	6) $\sqrt{2116}$ =

7) $\sqrt{2401}$ = 	8) $\sqrt{1849}$ = 	9) $\sqrt{1936}$ =

10) $\sqrt{2916}$ = 	11) $\sqrt{3249}$ = 	12) $\sqrt{3481}$ =

13) $\sqrt{4096}$ = 	14) $\sqrt{3721}$ = 	15) $\sqrt{4489}$ =

16) $\sqrt{5184}$ = 	17) $\sqrt{4761}$ = 	18) $\sqrt{4624}$ =

19) $\sqrt{5041}$ = 	20) $\sqrt{5329}$ =

Chapter 9

Multiplication Tables up to 100

About the Chapter

This chapter is about a very crucial topic called multiplication tables.

It begins with the basic understanding of multiplication tables, and explains the procedure to solve multiplication table related questions in detail.

It contains useful examples along with sufficient theory. It provides worksheets and exercises of various difficulty levels for practical, hands-on experience.

Multiplication Tables

A multiplication table is basically the multiplication of a specific number with the other different numbers. In other words, it is a table that shows us the results of multiplying two numbers.

Easily Calculate Multiplication Tables

Here, we will learn multiplication tables up to 100. The solution of this concept requires a two-step solution.

Step 1- First, we will multiply ones digit of the multiplier with the multiplicand and place it on the rightmost side of the answer.

Step 2- Then, we will multiply tens digit of the multiplier with the multiplicand and place it on the leftmost side of the answer.

Example 1: **Find 23x8.**

Solution 1: To find the product of the given numbers, we will:

S1- Multiply ones digit of the multiplier with the multiplicand and place it on the rightmost side of the answer.

3x8=24 (carry forward 2)

S2- Multiply tens digit of the multiplier with the multiplicand and place it on the leftmost side of the answer.

2x8=16; 16+2=18

Therefore, 23x8=184.

Hence solved.

 Find 44x6.

 To find the product of the given numbers, we will:

S1- Multiply ones digit of the multiplier with the multiplicand and place it on the rightmost side of the answer.

4x6=24 (4 will be placed at the rightmost side and 2 will be carried forward)

S2- Multiply tens digit of the multiplier with the multiplicand and place it on the leftmost side of the answer.

4x6=24; 24+2=26 (26 will be placed at the leftmost side)

Therefore, 44x6=264.

Hence solved.

 Find 52x8.

 To find the product of the given numbers, we will:

S1- Multiply ones digit of the multiplier with the multiplicand and place it on the rightmost side of the answer.

2x8=16 (6 will be placed at the rightmost side and 2 will be carried forward)

S2- Multiply tens digit of the multiplier with the multiplicand and place it on the leftmost side of the answer.

5x8=40; 40+1=41 (41 will be placed at the leftmost side)

Therefore, 52x8=416.

Hence solved.

 Find 33x7.

 To find the product of the given numbers, we will:

S1- Multiply ones digit of the multiplier with the multiplicand and place it on the rightmost side of the answer.

3x7=21 (1 will be placed at the rightmost side and 2 will be carried forward)

S2- Multiply tens digit of the multiplier with the multiplicand and place it on the leftmost side of the answer.

3x7=21; 21+2=23 (24 will be placed at the leftmost side)

Therefore, 33x7=231.

Hence solved.

 Find 93x6.

 To find the product of the given numbers, we will:

S1- Multiply ones digit of the multiplier with the multiplicand and place it on the rightmost side of the answer.

3x6=18 (8 will be placed at the rightmost side and 1 will be carried forward)

S2- Multiply tens digit of the multiplier with the multiplicand and place it on the leftmost side of the answer.

9x6=54; 54+1=55 (55 will be placed at the leftmost side)

Therefore, 93x6=558.

Hence solved.

 *Exercise 9.1*

Q1. Solve the following.

1)   26x2
2)   46x6
3)   58x9
4)   34x7
5)   67x3

Now, try to answer the questions of examples and exercise orally.

Example 6: **Find 32x8.**

Solution 6:

2x8=16

3x8=24; 24+1=25

Therefore, 32x8=256.

Hence solved.

Example 7: Find 43x5.

Solution 7:

3x5=15

4x5=20; 20+1=21

Therefore, 43x5=215.

Hence solved.

Example 8: **Find 55x6.**

Solution 8:

5x6=30

5x6=30; 30+3=33

Therefore, 55x6=330.

Hence solved.

Example 9: **Find 62x6.**

Solution 9:

2x6=12

6x6=36; 36+1=37

Therefore, 62x6=372

Hence solved.

Example 10: Find 75x5.

Solution 10:

5x5=25

7x5=35; 35+2=37

   Therefore, 75x5=375.

   Hence solved.

Exercise 9.2

Q1. Solve the following.

1)   39x9

2)   48x5

3)   52x8

4)   77x7

5)   60x6

WORKSHEET-12

Tables at a Glance

Q1. Match the following :

1)	45x6	496
2)	35x7	245
3)	53x6	270
4)	62x8	648
5)	72x9	318

Q2. Following the sums :

1) $22 \times 8 =$ 2) $23 \times 8 =$ 3) $18 \times 8 =$

4) $25 \times 9 =$ 5) $45 \times 6 =$ 6) $19 \times 9 =$

7) $73 \times 7 =$ 8) $92 \times 5 =$ 9) $44 \times 6 =$

10) $36 \times 8 =$ 11) $53 \times 6 =$ 12) $96 \times 6 =$

13) $22 \times 7 =$ 14) $63 \times 9 =$ 15) $56 \times 6 =$

16) $32 \times 6 =$ 17) $84 \times 8 =$ 18) $88 \times 8 =$

19) $73 \times 6 =$ 20) $92 \times 9 =$

Chapter 10 — Division

About the Chapter

This chapter is about division and the shortcut way to solve it.

It begins with the basic definition and knowledge of division. It then discusses about different categories of division-related questions and their solutions.

It provides theory as well as solved examples. Also, it has worksheets and exercises of various difficulty levels to test and improve student's performance.

Division

Division is one of the four main arithmetic operations of mathematics. Division basically means to split a large group into equal smaller groups or break a number into equal parts and find out how many equal parts can be made. For example, dividing 20 by 5 means splitting 20 into 5 equal groups of 4.

Usually, division is the most time-consuming and it is prone to many errors. But, with these easy and effective tricks, we can easily divide any number of any length quickly.

We will mostly focus on the specific division in this chapter. We will learn:

1) Division by 9
2) Division by 5
3) Division by 25
4) Division by 125
5) Below the base division

Division by 9

It is fairly easy to divide numbers by 9 using Vedic maths techniques.

Let us learn the right way to do it using examples.

> **Note:** The carry forward rule will be applicable and the carry forward will be on the LHS (previous digit).

Example 1: Divide 23242 by 9.

(To find the answer, we:

Step 1- Add the leftmost digit with the number to its right and keep doing this until we reach the second last digit [when the sum is greater than 9, carry forward to the previous digit].

Step 2- Add the sum obtained with the last digit and write it under the divisor.

Step 3- Divide both and write the remainder separately. Then add the carry forwards to get the final quotient.)

 To divide 23242 by 9, we will:

S1- Add 2 to 3, then their sum to 2 and continue till the second last digit (4).

2 (2+3) (2+3+2) (2+3+2+4)

2 5 7 1 (1 of 11 will be carried forward to the previous digit 7)

S2- Add the sum obtained (11) to the last digit (2) and write it under 9.

23242 by 9

2571   13 (11+2)

S3- Divide 13 by 9 to get the remainder and carry forward the quotient on the last digit (1) of 2571 and then add the carry forwards to get the final quotient.

13/9 gives 4 as the remainder.

2571

+ 11 (first 1 carried forward from 11, second 1 taken from the quotient of 13/9)

- -

2582 (final quotient)

Therefore, the quotient is 2582, and the remainder is 4.

Hence solved.

Example 2: **Divide 42322 by 9.**

 To divide 42322 by 9, we will:

S1- Add 4 to 2, then their sum to 3, and continue till the second last digit (2).

4 (4+2=6) (6+3=9) (9+2=11)

4 6 9 1 (carry forward 1 to previous digit 9)

S2- Add the sum obtained (11) to the last digit (2) and write it under 9.

42322 by 9

4691   13

S3- Divide 13 by 9 to get the remainder and carry forward the quotient on the last digit (1) of 4691 and then add the carry forwards to get the final quotient.

13/9 gives 4 as the remainder.

4691

+ 11

- -

4702 (final quotient)

Therefore, the quotient is 4702, and the remainder is 4.

Hence solved.

 *Exercise 10.1*

Q1. Divide the following.

1)   32423 by 9
2)   42524 by 9
3)   32423 by 9
4)   52123 by 9
5)   44552 by 9

Division by 5

To multiply a number with 5 we will simply multiply 2 by each digit and note down the product and then place a decimal before the unit digit of the number to get our final answer.

Let's look at some examples for a better understanding of the concept.

Example 3: **Divide 23422 by 5.**

(To get the answer, we:

Step 1 - Multiply each number by 2.

Step 2 - Place a decimal before the unit digit.)

Solution 3: To divide 23422 by 5, we will:

S1 - Multiply 23422 by 2.

23422

x   2
____

46844

S2 - Place a decimal before unit digit 4.

4684.4 (final answer)

Therefore, 23422/5 is 4684.4.

Hence solved.

Example 4: **Divide 42352 by 5.**

Solution 4: To divide 42352 by 5, we will:

S1 - Multiply 42352 by 2.

42352

x   2
____

84704

S2 - Place a decimal before unit digit 4.

8470.4 (final answer)

Therefore, 42352/5 is 8470.4.

Hence solved.

Vedic Maths

Exercise 10.2

Q1. Divide the following.

1)   63562 by 5
2)   32542 by 5
3)   42352 by 5
4)   54142 by 5
5)   24211 by 5

Division by 25

To divide a number 25, we will simply multiply 4 by each digit, and note down its product and then we will place a decimal before the tens digit of the number to get our final answer.

Let's look at some examples for a better understanding of the concept.

Example 5:   **Divide 32423 by 25.**

(To get the answer, we will:

Step 1 - Multiply the number by 4.

Step 2 - Place a decimal before the tens digit.)

Solution 5:   To divide 32423 by 25, we will:

S1 - Multiply 32423 by 4.

```
  32432
x     4
---------------
 129692
```

S2 - Place a decimal before the tens digit.

1296.92

Therefore, 32423/25=1296.92.

Hence solved.

Example 6:   **Divide 23672 by 25.**

Solution 6:   To divide 23672 by 25, we will:

S1 - Multiply 23672 by 4.

```
  23672
x     4
---------------
 94688
```

S2 - Place a decimal before the tens digit.

946.88

Therefore, 23672/25=946.88.

Hence solved.

Exercise 10.3

Q1. Divide the following.

1)   33254 by 25
2)   42234 by 25
3)   51515 by 25
4)   38917 by 25
5)   23451 by 25

Division by 125

To divide a number with 125, we will simply multiply it by 8, and note down its product and then we will place a decimal before the digit at the hundredths place to get our final answer.

Let's look at some examples for a better understanding of the concept.

Example 7: **Divide 22422 by 125.**

(To get the answer, we:

Step 1 - Multiply the number by 8.

Step 2 - Place a decimal before the hundreds digit.)

Solution 7:   To divide 22422 by 125, we will:

S1 - Multiply 22422 by 8.

```
   22422
x      8
-----------
  179376
```

S2 - Place a decimal before the tens digit.

179.376

Therefore, 22422/25=179.376.

Hence solved.

Example 8: **Divide 32423 by 125.**

Solution 8:   To divide 32423 by 125, we will:

S1 - Multiply 32423 by 8.

```
   32423
x      8
-----------
  259384
```

S2 - Place a decimal before the tens digit.

259.384

Therefore, 32423/125=259.384.

Hence solved.

Q1. Divide the following.

1)   42123 by 125
2)   22134 by 125
3)   54321 by 125
4)   39812 by 125
5)   55442 by 125

Below the Base Division

Every number has its base. A division is only possible if the divisor is smaller than the dividend. Here, we will learn how to divide the numbers which are smaller than their bases.

Let's learn this method using different examples.

Example 9:   **Divide 121314 by 99.**

(To find the answer, we will:

Step 1- Divide the dividend into two parts, i.e., quotient and remainder according to the base, from RHS.

Step 2- Take complement of the divisor and under quotient write down the first quotient digit as it is.

Step 3- Multiply it by the divisor, add the product with quotient, and continue doing this until the last digit.)

Solution 9:   **To divide 121314 by 99, we will:**

S1- Divide the dividend into two parts according to base, from RHS.

1213, 14

S2- Write down the complement of divisor (under divisor) and under the quotient column (below the line) write down the first quotient digit by making a proper structure.

The complement of 99 is 01 (100-99).

```
99 | 1213 | 14
01 |      |
   |______|____
    1   |
```

S3- Multiply the complement with the first quotient digit, then add the quotient column numbers and continue this process till the end.

We will write 1 as it is below the line, then multiply this 1 with 01 (complement of 99), then add 2 of 1213 with 0 of 01 (in line with it) and write it below the line (2).

Then, multiply this 2 with 01 and write it in the quotient column as shown. Then, in the quotient column, add 1 of 1213, 1 of 01, 0 of 02, and write the sum below the line (2).

Then, multiply 2 with 01 and write it in the quotient and remainder column. Then, in the quotient column add 3 of 1213, 2 of 02, 0 of 02, and write down the sum (5) below the line.

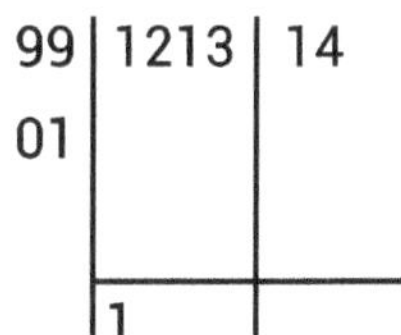

Then, multiply 5 with 01 and write it in the quotient remainder column as shown. Then, in the quotient column, add 1 of 14, 2 of 02, 0 of 05, and write the sum (3) below the line.

Lastly, add 4 of 14 and 5 of 05, and write the sum (9) below the line.

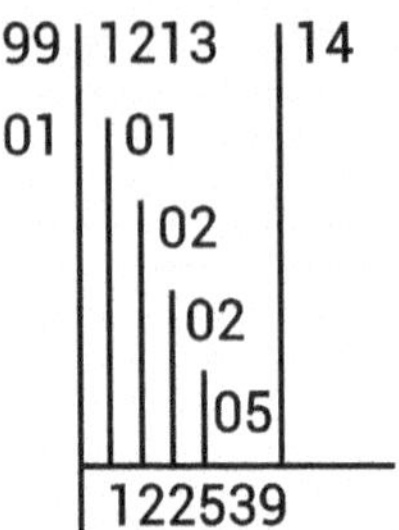

Therefore, the quotient is 1225, and the remainder is 39.

Hence solved.

Example 10: Divide 332211 by 99.

Solution 10: To divide 332211 by 99, we will:

S1- Divide the dividend into two parts according to base from RHS.

3322, 11

S2- Write down the complement of the divisor (under divisor) and under the quotient column (below the line) write down the first quotient digit by making a proper structure.

The complement of 99 is 01 (100-99).

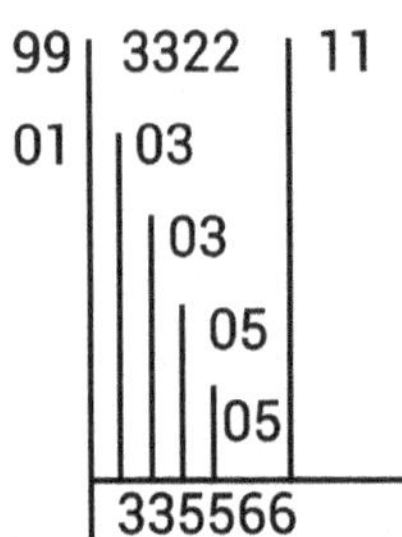

S3- Multiply the complement with the first quotient digit, then add the quotient column numbers and continue this process till the end.

Therefore, the quotient is 3355, and the remainder is 66.

Hence solved.

Example 11: Divide 121416 by 98.

Solution 11: To divide 121416 by 98, we will:

S1- Divide the dividend into two parts according to base, from RHS.

1214, 16

S2- Write down the complement of the divisor (under divisor) and under the quotient column (below the line) write down the first quotient digit by making a proper structure.

The complement of 98 is 02 (100-98).

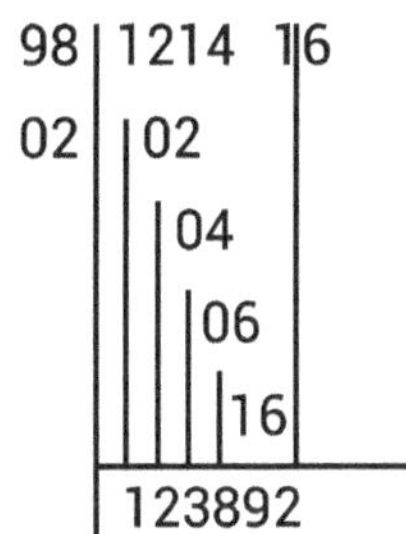

S3- Multiply the complement with the first quotient digit, then add the quotient column numbers and continue this process till the end.

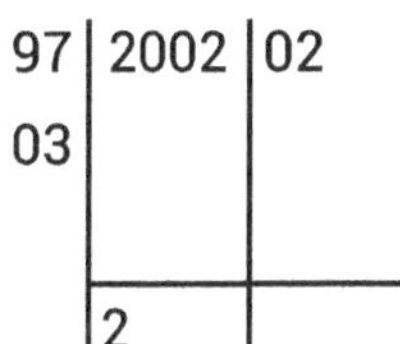

Therefore, the quotient is 1238, and the remainder is 92.

Hence solved.

Example 12: Divide 200202 by 97.

Solution 12: To divide 200202 by 97, we will:

S1- Divide the dividend into two parts according to base, from RHS.

2002, 02

S2- Write down the complement of the divisor (under divisor) and under the quotient column (below the line) write down the first quotient digit by making a proper structure.

The complement of 97 is 03 (100-97).

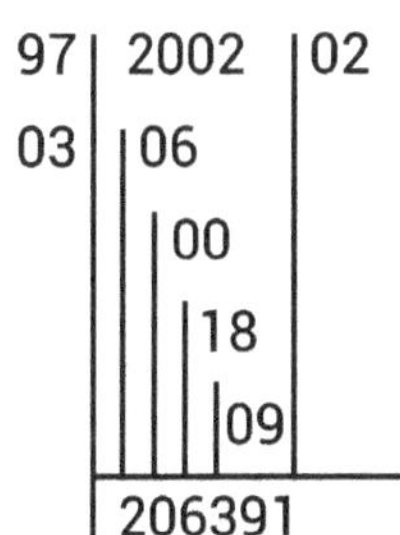

S3- Multiply the complement with the first quotient digit, then add the quotient column numbers and continue this process till the end.

97 | 2002 | 02
03 | 06
   | 00
   | 18
   | 09
___|______
   | 206391

Therefore, the quotient is 2063, and the remainder is 91.

Hence solved.

Example 13: Divide 531827 by 96.

 To divide 531827 by 96, we will:

S1- Divide the dividend into two parts according to base, from RHS.

5318, 27

S2- Write down the complement of the divisor (under divisor) and under the quotient column (below the line) write down the first quotient digit by making a proper structure.

The complement of 96 is 04 (100-96).

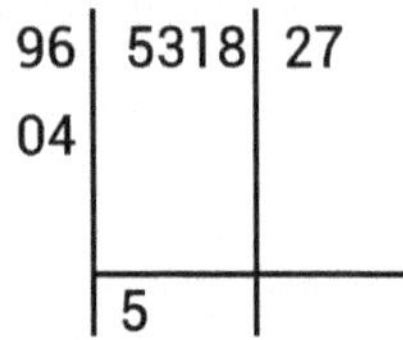

S3- Multiply the complement with the first quotient digit, then add the quotient column numbers and continue this process till the end.

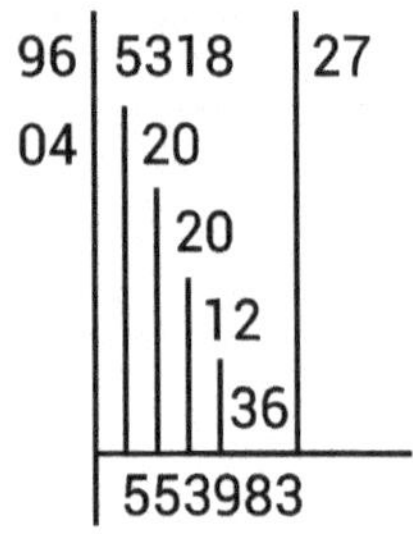

Therefore, the quotient is 5539, and the remainder is 83.

Hence solved.

Example 14: Divide 630257 by 993.

Solution 14: To divide 630257 by 993, we will:

S1- Divide the dividend into two parts according to base, from RHS.

630, 257

S2- Write down the complement of the divisor (under divisor) and under the quotient column (below the line) write down the first quotient digit by making a proper structure.

The complement of 993 is 007 (1000-993).

993 | 630 | 257
007 | |
    | 6 |

S3- Multiply the complement with the first quotient digit, then add the quotient column numbers and continue this process till the end.

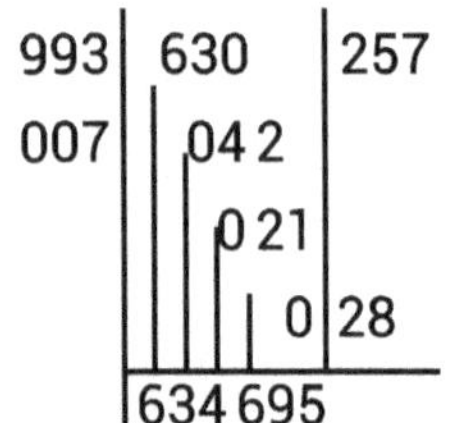

Therefore, the quotient is 634, and the remainder is 695.

Hence solved.

 *Exercise 10.4*

Q1. Divide the following.

1)   412345 by 99
2)   231212 by 98
3)   541678 by 97
4)   332289 by 995
5)   561230 by 993

WORKSHEET-13

Q1. Quick Division by 9

1) $223212 \div 9 =$	2) $121231 \div 9 =$	3) $211202 \div 9 =$
4) $224031 \div 9 =$	5) $321211 \div 9 =$	6) $103452 \div 9 =$
7) $112233 \div 9 =$	8) $131224 \div 9 =$	9) $321103 \div 9 =$
10) $401132 \div 9 =$		

Q2. Quick Division by 5, 25, 125

1) $431211 \div 5 =$	2) $421231 \div 5 =$	3) $221232 \div 5 =$
4) $254021 \div 5 =$	5) $322441 \div 25 =$	6) $123452 \div 25 =$
7) $422331 \div 25 =$	8) $323452 \div 25 =$	9) $433442 \div 125 =$
10) $323453 \div 125 =$	11) $522332 \div 125 =$	12) $123242 \div 125 =$

Q3. Division by Numbers below the base

1) 2403 ÷ 99 =   2) 11023 ÷ 97 =   3) 2732 ÷ 99 =

4) 42301 ÷ 996 =   5) 93678 ÷ 991 =   6) 53064 ÷ 93=

7) 45962 ÷ 93 =   8) 39854 ÷ 9989 =

11 Digital Roots

About the Chapter

This chapter is devoted to the study of digital roots, which is an unknown yet unique and extremely useful topic to check the answers.

This chapter begins with the basic definition and knowledge of digital roots. Then, the chapter informs about how to use it to check the answers of various arithmetic operations.

This chapter is well supplemented with examples with their detailed solutions. It also contains exercises and worksheets for practice.

Digital Root

A Perfect Answer Checking Tool

A digital root is a single-digit positive integer (1 to 9). It cannot be zero or negative. And it is used to check whether the answer is right or wrong.

We will first learn how to calculate the digital root of any number; then, we will learn its applications.

Calculation of Digital Root (DR).

To calculate digital root, we have two tricks: normal trick and magical trick. We will learn these tricks step by step.

1)   Normal Trick

In the normal trick, to calculate the DR, we will add digits of number from left to right till it becomes a single-digit number. Let us understand using illustrations.

2)   Magical Trick

Here, we will proceed in the similar manner and add all digits to get the DR, but we will ignore 9. If the sum of digits becomes 9 or 9 itself appears, then we will cast out 9. If the sum comes out to be 0, we will take final DR as 9 and not 0. Let's understand using examples.

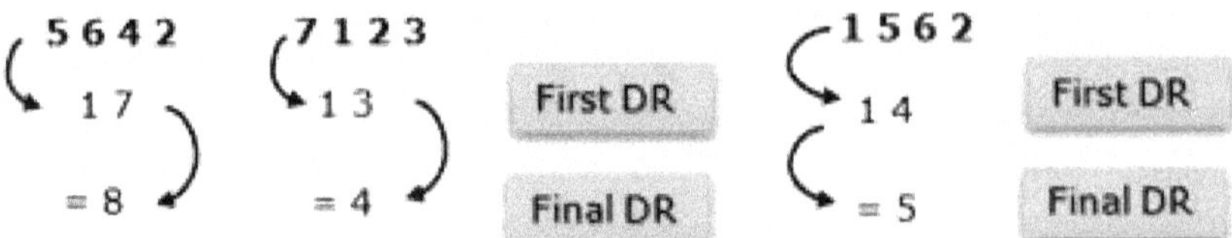

- 364

  As 3+6=9, so we will cast out 9.

  (3+6+4)

  DR=4

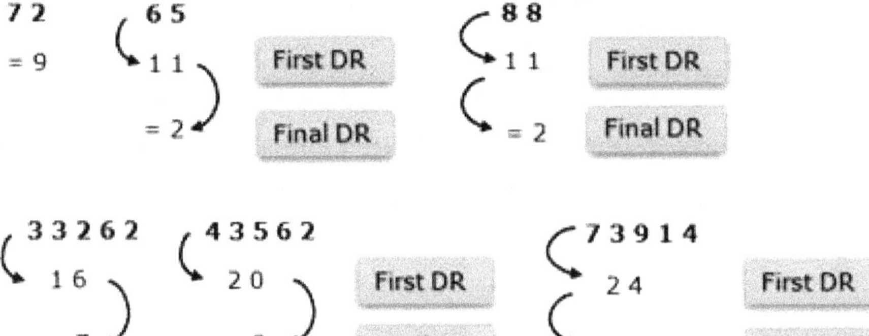

- 954

As 9 is there, so will cast it out and as 5+4=9, we will cast it out as well. So, we are left with 0, but we will put the DR as 9 as per standard rules.

9+5+4

DR=9

Applications of Digital Root (DR).

We can apply the DR to cross-check the answers of our basic arithmetic operations, i.e., addition, subtraction, multiplication and square related problems. The process to cross-check is the same for all operations. It contains three steps.

Step 1- Calculate the DR of numbers given in the question.

Step 2- Do arithmetical operation (addition/subtraction/multiplication/squaring) on the DR of question as per given problem.

Step 3- Match the answer of Step 2 with the DR of the answer. If it is equal, then our answer will be right; otherwise, it will be wrong.

1. Addition

Example 1: **Check whether the sum of 6345, 9878, 6354, 9679 is 32256 or not.**

(To check this, we will:

Step 1- Find the DR of each number.

Step 2- Add the DRs of all numbers.

Step 3- Compare the DR of the answer with Step 2 result.)

Solution 1: To check the sum, we will:

S1- Find the DR of each number.

DR of 6345=6+3+4+5=9 (by casting out 9 technique)

DR of 9878=9+8+7+8=23=2+3=5

DR of 6354=6+3+5+4=9

DR of 9679=9+6+7+9=13=1+3=4

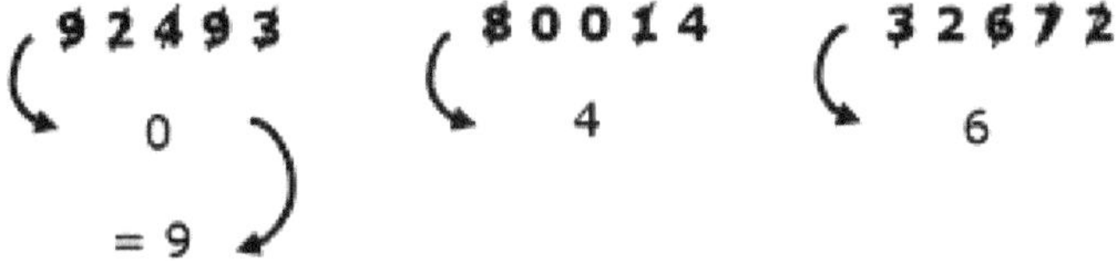

S2- Add the DRs of all numbers.

9+5+9+4=27

=2+7

=9

S3- Compare the DR of the given answer with the Step 2 result.

DR of answer=3+2+2+5+6=9

As this is equal to S2 result, therefore the sum is correct.

Hence solved.

Example 2: **Check whether the sum of 7254, 3896, 6245, 3127 is 20532 or not.**

Solution 2: To check the sum, we will:

S1- Find the DR of each number.

S2- Add the DRs of all numbers.

S3- Compare the DR of the given answer with the Step 2 result.

As both DRs are different, therefore it is incorrect.

Hence solved.

Exercise 11.1

Q1. Find the sum and check it using the DR technique.

1)   3674, 9854, 3678, 9254

2)   5412, 8789, 2352, 5414

3)   4422, 7653, 4422, 5649

4)   2389, 8763, 1947, 9542

5)   5382, 3452, 2323, 5382

2. Subtraction

Example 3:   Check whether the subtraction result of 726354 and 289673 is 436681 or not.

Solution 3:   To check it, we will:

S1- Find the DR of each number.

DR of 726354=7+2+6+3+5+4=9

DR of 289673=2+8+9+6+7+3=8

S2- Subtract the DRs of both numbers.

9-8=1

S3- Compare the DR of the given answer with the Step 2 result.

DR of the given answer 436681=4+3+6+6+8+1=10=1

=1+0

=1

As the DRs of both are the same, therefore it is correct.

Hence solved.

$$
\begin{array}{cccccc}
 & 7 & 2 & 6 & 3 & 5 & 4 \\
- & 2 & 8 & 9 & 6 & 7 & 3 \\
\hline
 & 4 & 3 & 6 & 6 & 8 & 1
\end{array}
$$

	D R
	0 9
−	8
	1

As shown, DR gives **1** and check ✓, **1**.

Example 4: Check whether the subtraction result of 386748 and 193689 is 193059 or not.

Solution 4: To check it, we will:

S1- Find the DR of each number.

S2- Subtract the DRs of both numbers.

S3- Compare DR of the given answer with the Step 2 result.

As the DRs of both are the same, therefore it is correct.

Exercise 11.2

Q1. Find the sum and check it using the DR technique.

1)   3674, 9854, 3678, 9254
2)   5412, 8789, 2352, 5414
3)   4422, 7653, 4422, 5649
4)   2389, 8763, 1947, 9542
5)   5382, 3452, 2323, 5382

Example 5: Check whether the multiplication result of 634 and 243 is 154062 or not.

Solution 5: To check it, we will:

S1- Find the DR of each number.

DR of 6+3+4=4

DR of 243=2+4+3=9

S2- Multiply the DRs of both numbers.

4x9=36

Vedic Maths

S3- Compare the DR of the given answer with the Step 2 result.

DR of 154062=1+5+4+0+6+2=9

As the DRs of both are the same, therefore it is correct.

Hence solved.

Example 6: Check whether the subtraction result of 862 and 145 is 125990 or not.

Solution 6: To check it, we will:

S1- Find the DR of each number.

S2- Multiply the DRs of both numbers.

S3- Compare the DR of the given answer with the Step 2 result.

As the DRs of both are different, therefore it is incorrect.

Hence solved.

Exercise 11.3

Q1. Multiply the numbers and check the answer.

1)   639 and 123
2)   345 and 543
3)   123 and 873
4)   909 and 738
5)   444 and 888

Example 7: Check whether the square of 63 is 3969 or not.

Solution 7: To check it, we will:

S1- Find the DR of both numbers.

DR of 63=6+3=9

DR of 63=6+3=9

S2- Multiply the DRs of both numbers.

9x9=81

=8+1

=9

S3- Compare the DR of the given answer with the Step 2 result.

DR of 3969=3+9+6+9=9

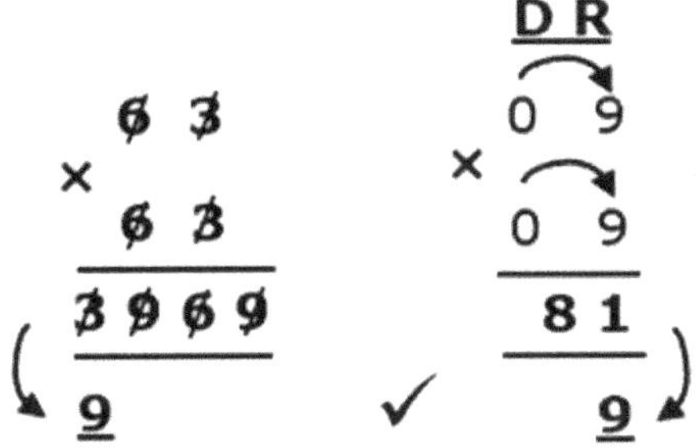

As the DRs of both are the same, therefore it is correct.   Hence solved.

Example 8: Check whether the square of 78 is 6084 or   not.

Solution 8: To check it, we will:

S1- Find the DR of both numbers.

S2- Multiply the DRs of both numbers.

S3- Compare the DR of the given answer with the Step 2 result.

```
        D R
7 8     15 6
  x7 8      15 6
6084    36 9
 9        9
```

As the DRs of both are the same, therefore it is correct.

Hence solved.

Q1. Square the number and check the answer.

1) 34
2) 55
3) 76
4) 89
5) 27

WORKSHEET-14

Digital Roots

Q1. Find the Digital Root (DR)

1) 23 DR =	2) 26 DR =	3) 12 DR =
4) 35 DR =	5) 96 DR =	6) 87 DR =
7) 68 DR =	8) 45 DR =	9) 97 DR =
10) 77 DR =	11) 242 DR =	12) 453 DR =
13) 622 DR =	14) 433 DR =	15) 712 DR =
16) 435 DR =	17) 613 DR =	18) 546 DR =
19) 913 DR =	20) 543 DR =	21) 2423 DR =

Q2. Verify whether the following answer are correct or not using Digital Root (DR)

1) 3263 + 1594 = 4857 =	2) 4443 + 2375 = 6818 =
3) 5183 + 2463 = 7645 =	4) 4390 + 5399 = 9289 =
5) 4273 + 2645 = 6928 =	6) 6031 + 2486 = 8517 =
7) 1537 + 6298 = 7825 =	8) 3571 + 2283 = 5854 =
9) 2354 + 2454 = 4608 =	10) 1469 + 2845 = 4314 =

Vedic Maths

Q2. Verify whether the following answer are correct or not using Digital Root (DR)

1) 4654 - 3295 = 1349 =   2) 7644 - 2981 = 4663 =

3) 5948 - 2876 = 3172 =   4) 6745 - 3892 = 2853 =

5) 7649 - 2987 = 4622 =   6) 4893 - 3589 = 1314 =

7) 9345 - 8123 = 1212 =   8) 8843 - 3592 = 5221 =

9) 7948 - 3897 = 4051 =   10) 8043 - 5958 = 2085 =

Q3. Verify whether the following answer are correct or not using Digital Root (DR)

1) $313 \times 224 = 70112 =$ 2) $224 \times 513 = 114912 =$

3) $332 \times 228 = 75646 =$ 4) $323 \times 232 = 74926 =$

5) $432 \times 226 = 97632 =$ 6) $323 \times 232 = 74126 =$

Q4. Verify whether the following answer are correct or not using Digital Root (DR)

1) $56^2 = 2116 =$ 2) $63^2 = 3969 =$

3) $78^2 = 6284 =$ 4) $69^2 = 4861 =$

5) $44^2 = 1936 =$ 6) $62^2 = 3844 =$

Cube Roots

About the Chapter

This chapter is about shortcut ways to find cube roots.

It begins with the basic understanding of the cube root. And teaches how to calculate it without using pen and paper.

The chapter includes theory along with different examples, which makes this complicated topic much easier to understand and implement.

The chapter contains useful exercises and worksheets for practice and self-assessment.

Cube Root

A cube root is the reverse of a cube. That means the parent number of a cube is known as its cube root. It can also be understood as a value that produces the original value when multiplied by itself thrice. For example, the cube root of 64, denoted as $\sqrt[3]{64}$, is 4, because when we multiply 4 by itself three times, we get 4x4x4=64=4^3.

The traditional cube root calculation method, in general, is very long, complicated, and it is prone to various mistakes. But with a short and easy trick, cube root calculation can be made extremely simple. To understand the technique, it is essential for us to learn cubes till 9.

Numbers	Cubes
1^3	1
2^3	8
3^3	27
4^3	64
5^3	125
6^3	216
7^3	343
8^3	512
9^3	729

Table 12.1: Numbers and their cubes

Calculate Cube Roots Easily

To calculate a cube root, we will first divide the cube into two parts. This segregation will be done from RHS, and the RHS number should compulsorily have three digits.

Then we will solve the LHS number. For that, we will find the nearest cube number, which is either less than or equal to the LHS number. Now to calculate the RHS value, we will have two options. When the unit digit is:

1)   4, 5, 6, 9, 1, or 0, we will write it as is.

2)   8, 2, 7, or 3, we will write its complement.

Then we will combine the LHS and RHS numbers to get our cube root. Let us look at some examples to understand the topic further.

Example 12.1:   **Find the cube root of 117649.**

(To get the answer, we will:

Step 1- Divide the given number into two parts from the RHS.

Step 2- Find the nearest cube number to the LHS number to get the LHS part of the answer.

Step 3- Write the number as it is if the last digit of the RHS number is 4, 5, 6, 9, 1, or 0. Else, if it is 2, 3, 7, or 8, we will write its complement to get the RHS part of the answer.)

Solution 12.1:   To find the cube root, we will:

S1- Divide the given number into two parts from RHS.

117|649

S2- Find the nearest cube number to the LHS number to get the LHS part of the answer.

Cube of 4 (64)<117<Cube of 5 (125)

Therefore, we will consider 4 as our LHS part of the answer.

S3- Find the RHS part of the answer.

As the last digit is 9, so 9 will be our RHS part of the answer.

Therefore, the answer is 49.

Hence solved.

Example 12.2:   **Find the cube root of 778688.**

Solution 12.2:   To find the cube root, we will:

S1- Divide the given number into two parts from the RHS.

778|688

S2- Find the nearest cube number to the LHS number to get the LHS part of the answer.

Cube of 9 (729)<778<Cube of 10 (1000)

Therefore, we will consider 9 as our LHS part of the answer.

S3- Find the RHS part of the answer.

As the last digit is 8, so we will take the complement of it.

Complement of 8=2 (10-8). So, 2 will be our RHS part of the answer.

Therefore, the answer is 92.

Hence solved.

Example 12.3: **Find the cube root of 12167.**

Solution 12.3: To find the cube root, we will:

S1- Divide the given number into two parts from the RHS.

12|167

S2- Find the nearest cube number to the LHS number to get the LHS part of the answer.

Cube of 2 (8)<12<Cube of 3 (27)

Therefore, we will consider 2 as our LHS part of the answer.

S3- Find the RHS part of the answer.

As the last digit is 7, so we will take the complement of it.

Complement of 7=3 (10-7). So, 3 will be our RHS part of the answer.

Therefore, the answer is 23.

Hence solved.

Example 12.4: **Find the cube root of 42875.**

Solution 12.4: To find the cube root, we will:

S1- Divide the given number into two parts from the RHS.

42|875

S2- Find the nearest cube number to the LHS number to get the LHS part of the answer.

The nearest cube number is 3.

S3- Find the RHS part of the answer.

The last digit is 5, so it will be the RHS part.

Therefore, the answer is 35.

Hence solved.

Example 12.5: **Find the cube root of 54872.**

Solution 12.5: To find the cube root, we will:

S1- Divide the given number into two parts from the RHS.

54|872

S2- Find the nearest cube number to the LHS number to get the LHS part of the answer.

The nearest cube number is 3.

S3- Find the RHS part of the answer.

The last digit is 2, so 10-2=8 will be the RHS part.

Therefore, the answer is 38.

Hence solved.

Exercise 12.1

Q1. Find the cube root of the following.

1) 941192
2) 704969
3) 531441
4) 389017
5) 216000

Example 12.6: **Find the cube root of 117649.**

Solution 12.6: To find the cube root, we will:

S1- Divide the given number into two parts from the RHS.

117|649

S2- Find the nearest cube number to the LHS number to get the LHS part of the answer.

The nearest cube number is 4.

S3- Find the RHS part of the answer.

The last digit is 9, so it will be the RHS part.

Therefore, the answer is 49.

Hence solved.

Example 12.7: **Find the cube root of 132651.**

Solution 12.7: To find the cube root, we will:

S1- Divide the given number into two parts from the RHS.

132|651

S2- Find the nearest cube number to the LHS number to get the LHS part of the answer.

The nearest cube number is 5.

S3- Find the RHS part of the answer.

The last digit is 1, so it will be the RHS part.

Therefore, the answer is 51.

Hence solved.

Example 12.8: **Find the cube root of 103823.**

Solution 12.8: To find the cube root, we will:

S1- Divide the given number into two parts from the RHS.

103|823

S2- Find the nearest cube number to the LHS number to get the LHS part of the answer.

The nearest cube number is 4.

S3- Find the RHS part of the answer.

The last digit is 3, so 10-3=7 will be the RHS part.

Therefore, the answer is 47.

Hence solved.

Example 12.9: **Find the cube root of 571787.**

Solution 12.9: To find the cube root, we will:

S1- Divide the given number into two parts from the RHS.

571|787

S2- Find the nearest cube number to the LHS number to get the LHS part of the answer.

The nearest cube number is 8.

S3- Find the RHS part of the answer.

The last digit is 7, so 10-7=3 will be the RHS part.

Therefore, the answer is 83.

Hence solved.

Example 12.10: **Find the cube root of 729000.**

Solution 12.10: To find the cube root, we will:

S1- Divide the given number into two parts from the RHS.

729|000

S2- Find the nearest cube number to the LHS number to get the LHS part of the answer.

The nearest cube number is 9.

S3- Find the RHS part of the answer.

The last digit is 0, so it will be the RHS part.

Therefore, the answer is 90.

Hence solved.

 *Exercise 12.2*

Q1. Find the cube root of the following.

1)   884736
2)   140608
3)   636056
4)   274625
5)   970299

WORKSHEET-15

Q1. Find the cubes roots of the following perfect cubes :

1) $\sqrt[3]{778688}$ =

2) $\sqrt[3]{551368}$ =

3) $\sqrt[3]{205379}$ =

4) $\sqrt[3]{24389}$ =

5) $\sqrt[3]{857375}$ =

6) $\sqrt[3]{592704}$ =

7) $\sqrt[3]{50653}$ =

8) $\sqrt[3]{17576}$ =

9) $\sqrt[3]{941192}$ =

10) $\sqrt[3]{636056}$ =

11) $\sqrt[3]{166375}$ =

12) $\sqrt[3]{6859}$ =

13) $\sqrt[3]{804357}$ =

14) $\sqrt[3]{681472}$ =

15) $\sqrt[3]{125000}$ =

16) $\sqrt[3]{4096}$ =

17) $\sqrt[3]{912673}$ =

18) $\sqrt[3]{704969}$ =

19) $\sqrt[3]{195112}$ =

20) $\sqrt[3]{157464}$ =

13 Divisibility of Prime Numbers

About the Chapter

This chapter is related to the divisibility of prime numbers, which is an essential topic for competitive exams.

It begins with the basic information of divisibility tests for different numbers. Then, it goes on to explain the concept of osculators, which are helpful in checking the divisibility of more numbers.

It is well supplemented with theory and examples. Also, it contains exercises and worksheets of various difficulty levels.

Divisibility Tests of Numbers

A Single Table Solution

Number	Divisibility Test	Examples
2	The last digit of the number should be even or 0.	324672 is divisible by 2 as the last digit is even.
3	The digital root of the number should be 3, 6, or 9.	6337233 is divisible by 3 as the DR is 9.
4	The last two digits should be divisible by 4.	423612 is divisible by 4 as 12 is divisible by 4.
5	The last digit should be 0 or 5.	736740 is divisible by 5 as the last digit is 0.
6	The number should be divisible by 2 and 3.	362434 is not divisible by 6 as it is not divisible by 3.
8	The last three digits should be divisible by 8.	673512 is divisible by 8 as 512 is divisible by 8.
9	The digital root of the number should be 9.	726354 is divisible by 9 as the DR is 9.

Number	Divisibility Test	Examples
10	The last digit should be 0.	367240 is divisible by 10 as the last digit is 0.
12	The number should be divisible by 3 and 4.	846060 is divisible by 12 as it is divisible by 3 and 4.
15	The number should be divisible by 3 and 5.	934635 is divisible by 15 as it is divisible by 3 and 5.
18	The number should be divisible by 2 and 9.	as not divisible by 18 as it is 762432 not divisible by 9.

Table 13.1: Divisibility test for some numbers.

Check divisibility using Osculation process

Osculation is a Vedic math technique to quickly determine if a number is evenly divisible by any divisor or not. There are two types of osculators: positive osculators and negative osculators.

The positive osculator comes into play when the divisor has 9 at its unit digit. For example, 169, 19, 49, 102589, etc. However, a negative osculator comes into the picture when the divisor has 1 at its unit digit. For example, 11, 21, 251, 265481, etc.

Let's understand what exactly osculators are and how to use them to check the divisibility of numbers.

Find the Osculator Smoothly

Positive Osculator

To calculate a positive osculator, we will simply remove the unit digit and replace it with the next occurring number, using the buy 1 more than the one before rule.

Any divisor whose unit digit as 7 or 3 can be converted into a positive osculator by multiplying 3 or 7 with it, making its unit place as 9 or 1. We will understand its various uses afterward. First, let's understand this concept using examples.

Example 1: Find the osculator of 69.

(To find it, we will:

Step 1 - Drop the unit digit.

Step 2 - Use buy one more than one before rule, i.e., increase the digit by one.)

Solution 1: To find the osculator, we will:

S1 - Drop the unit digit, 9.

S2 - Add one to the remaining number.

Therefore, the osculator is 7.

Hence solved.

Solution 2: To find the osculator, we will:

S1- Drop the unit digit 9.

S2- Add one to the remaining number.

Therefore, the osculator is 13.

Hence solved.

Example 3: Find the osculator of 99.

Solution 3: To find the osculator, we will:

S1- Drop the unit digit 9.

S2- Add one to the remaining number.

Therefore, the osculator is 10.

Hence solved.

Example 4: Find the osculator of 7.

Solution 4: Osculator of 7 can be found using both positive and negative osculation processes. But generally, we will prefer the positive process for this.

To find the osculator, we will:

S1- Multiply the last digit with the complete number.

S2- Drop the last number.

S3- Add one to the remaining number.

7x7=49

Drop 9, add one to 4.

Therefore, the osculator is 5.

Hence solved.

Example 5: Find the osculator of 43.

Solution 5: Osculator of a number ending with 3 can be found using both positive and negative osculation processes. But generally, we will prefer the positive process for this.

To find the osculator, we will:

S1- Multiply the last digit with complete number.

S2- Drop the last number.

S3- Add one to the remaining number.

43x3=129

Drop 9, add one to 12.

Therefore, the osculator is 13.

Hence solved.

 *Exercise 13.1*

Q1. Find the osculator of the following.

1)   89

2)   139

3)   37

4)   93

5)   157

Negative Osculator

To calculate a negative osculator, we will simply remove its unit digit and keep the rest of the number same.

Example 6:   **Find the osculator of 321.**

(To find it, we:

Step 1 - Drop the unit digit.

Step 2 - Write the remaining number as it is.)

Solution 6:   To find the osculator, we will:

S1 - Drop the unit digit 1.

S2 - Write the remaining number as it is.

Therefore, the osculator is 32.

Hence solved.

Example 7:   **Find the osculator of 111.**

Solution 7:   To find the osculator, we will:

S1 - Drop the unit digit 1.

S2 - Write the remaining number as it is.

Therefore, the osculator is 11.

Hence solved.

Example 8:   **Find the negative osculator of 7.**

Solution 8:   To find the osculator, we will:

S1 - Multiply the number by 3 to make the last digit 1.

S2 - Drop the last number.

S3 - Write the remaining number as it is.

7x3=21

Drop 1, write remaining as it is.

Therefore, the osculator is 2.

Example 9:   **Find the negative osculator of 37.**

Solution 9:   To find the osculator, we will:

S1- Multiply the number by 3 to make the last digit 1.

S2- Drop the last number.

S3- Write the remaining number as it is.

37x3=111

Drop 1, write remaining as it is.

Therefore, the osculator is 11.

Hence solved.

Example 10:	**Find the negative osculator of 13.**

Solution 10:	To find the osculator, we will:

S1- Multiply the number by 7 to make the last digit 1.

S2- Drop the last number.

S3- Write the remaining number as it is.

13x7=91

Drop 1, write remaining as it is.

Therefore, the osculator is 9.

Hence solved.

Exercise 13.2

Q1. Find the osculator of the following.

1)   71
2)   131
3)   87
4)   53
5)   123

Application of Osculators

Positive Osculator

To check the divisibility using a positive osculator, we will follow these steps:

1.   Multiply the positive osculator by the unit digit of the divisor and add it with the tens digit.

2.   Follow the same steps for other digits also, from right to left.

3.   In the case of a double-digit number, write the number and multiply the osculator with the unit digit of the divisor and add the rest of the digit to it.

4.   Then, add the sum received from the previous step and the immediate left number and note its sum.

5.   If the final digit obtained is the same as the dividend, then the number will be divisible by the divisor.

Example 11: Check if 17423 is divisible by 19 or not using the positive osculation process.

(To check this, we:

Step 1- Find the positive osculator.

Step 2- Multiply the osculator by the last digit, then add it to the previous digit and repeat the same.

Solution 11: To check it, we will:

S1- Find the positive osculator.

Drop 9, add one to the remaining number.

Therefore, the positive osculator of 19 will be 2.

S2- Multiply osculator (2) by the last digit (3 of 17423), then add it to the previous digit (2 of 17423) and repeat the same for the rest of the number.

2x3+2=8

2x8+4=20

As it is a two-digit number, we will multiply the last number with positive osculate that we found and then add it to the next digit of two-digit number. And then add it to the next digit of the main number.

2x0=0; 0+2=2

2+7=9

Continue the same process of multiplication and addition.

2x9+1=19

As the last number is 19, which is equal to the divisor, therefore, the given number is divisible by 19.

Hence solved.

Example 12: Check if 324232 is divisible by 19 or not using the positive osculation process.

Solution 12: To check it, we will:

S1- Find the positive osculator.

Drop 9, add one to the remaining number.

Therefore, the positive osculator of 19 will be 2.

S2- Multiply osculator (2) by last digit (2 of 324232), then add it to the previous digit (3 of 324232) and repeat the same for the other digits.

2x2+3=7

2x7+2=16

As it is a two-digit number, we will multiply it then add it to another digit, as we did in the previous example.

2x6+1=13

13+4=17 (two-digit number)

2x7=14+1=15

15+2=17 (two-digit number)

2x7=14+1=15

15+3=18

As the last number is 18, it does not match with 19. So, 324232 is not divisible by 19.

Hence solved.

Example 12: Check if 92423 is divisible by 29 or not using the positive osculation process.

Solution 12: To check it, we will:

S1- Find the positive osculator.

Drop 9, add one to the remaining number.

Therefore, the positive osculator of 29 will be 3.

S2- Multiply osculator by the last digit, then add it to the previous digit and repeat the same for the other digits.

3x3+2=11 (two-digit number)

3x1+1=4

4+4=8

3x8+2=26 (two-digit number)

3x6=18+2=20

20+9=29

As it is the same as the divisor, therefore the given number is divisible by 29.

Hence solved.

Example 13: Check if 27426 is divisible by 13

or not using the positive osculation process.

Solution 13: To check it, we will:

S1- Find the positive osculator.

Multiply the last digit with the complete number, drop the last digit, and add one to the remaining.

13x3=39

Therefore, the positive osculator of 13 will be 4.

S2- Multiply osculator by the last digit, then add it to the previous digit and repeat the same for the other digits.

4x6+2=26

6x4+2=26

26+4=30

4x0=0+3=3

3+7=10

4x0=0+1=1

1+2=3

Therefore, it is not divisible by 13.

Hence solved.

Q1. Check the divisibility of the following.

1. 232423 by 19
2. 32423 by 29
3. 45423 by 49
4. 32423 by 59
5. 93148 by 17

Negative Osculator

To check the divisibility using the negative osculator, we will follow these steps:

Multiply the negative osculator by the unit digit of the divisor and add it with the tens digit.

Follow the same steps for the other digits, from right to left.

In the case of a double-digit number, write the number and multiply the osculator by the unit digit of the divisor and add the rest of the digit to it.

Then, add the sum received in the previous step and the immediate left number and note its sum. If there is bar over the number, then subtract it.

If we get 0, multiple of the divisor, or a number similar to the divisor as the final answer, then the given number will be divisible by the divisor.

Example 14: **Check if 84651 is divisible by 21**

or not using the negative osculation process.

(To check it, we will:

Step 1- Find the negative osculator.

Step 2- Put bar over alternative digits to represent the negative osculation.

Step 3- Follow the same step as done in the positive osculation, but rather than adding, subtract the numbers.)

Solution 14: To check it, we will:

S1- Find the negative osculator.

Drop the last digit, write the remaining as it is.

The negative osculator of 21 will be 2.

S2- Put bar over alternative digits to represent negative osculation.

8 4̄ 6 5̄ 1

S3- Follow the same step as done in positive osculation, but rather than addition, subtract from the numbers which have bars over them.

Multiply the last digit of the given number by the negative osculator.

2x1=2

Next number is 5 , which means negative 5. Therefore, we will subtract it.

2-5=-3=3̄

2x-3=-6=6

-6+6=0

2x0=0

0-4=-4=4

2x-4=-8=8

-8+8=0

As the final number is 0, therefore it is divisible by 21.

Hence solved.

 Check if 404395 is divisible by 31

or not using the negative osculation process.

 To check it, we will:

S1- Find the negative osculator.

Drop the last digit, write the remaining as it is.

The negative osculator of 31 will be 3.

S2- Put bar over alternative digits to represent negative osculation.

4 04 39 5

S3- Follow the same step as done in positive osculation, but rather than addition, subtract from the numbers which have bars.

3x5=15

15-9=6

3x6=18

18+3=21 (two-digit number)

3x1-2=1

1-4=-3

3x-3=-9=9

-9+0=-9=9

3x-9=-27=(27)

-27-4=-31=(31)

Therefore, it is divisible by 31.

Hence solved.

Try with Both Methods

Let's try to check the divisibility of the same number using the positive and negative osculation processes.

Positive Process

 Check if 24836 is divisible by 7

or not using the positive osculation process.

2x-3=-6=6

-6+6=0

2x0=0

0-4=-4=4

2x-4=-8=8

-8+8=0

As the final number is 0, therefore it is divisible by 21.

Hence solved.

 Check if 404395 is divisible by 31 Solution 16: To check it, we will:

S1- Find the positive osculator.

Multiply by 7, drop the last digit, and add one to the remaining number.

7x7=49; 4+1=5

Therefore, the positive osculator of 7 will be 5.

S2- Multiply the osculator by the last digit, then add it to the next digit and repeat the same for the other digits.

5x6+3=33

5x3+3=18

18+8=26

5x6+2=32

32+4=36

5x6+2=32

32+4=36

5x6+3=33

33+2=35

As 35 is divisible by 7, therefore, 24836 is divisible by 7.

Hence solved.

Negative Process

 Check if 24836 is divisible by 7 or not using the negative osculation process.

 To check it, we will:

S1- Find the negative osculator.

Multiply 7 by 3 to get 1 in unit place, drop the last digit, and write the remaining number as it is.

7x3=21

Therefore, the negative osculator will be 2.

S2- Put bar over alternative digits to represent negative osculation.

24 83 6

S3- Follow the same step as done in positive osculation, but rather than addition, subtract from the numbers which have bars over them.

2x6=12

12-3=9

2x9=18

18+8=26

2x6=12-2=10

10-4=6

2x6=12

12+2=14

As 14 is divisible by 7, therefore, 24836 is divisible by 7.

Hence solved.

or not using the negative osculation process.

 To check it, we will:

S1- Find the negative osculator.

Drop the last digit, write the remaining as it is.

The negative osculator of 31 will be 3.

S2- Put bar over alternative digits to represent negative osculation.

4 04 39 5

S3- Follow the same step as done in positive osculation, but rather than addition, subtract from the numbers which have bars.

3x5=15

15-9=6

3x6=18

18+3=21 (two-digit number)

3x1-2=1

1-4=-3

3x-3=-9=9

-9+0=-9=9

3x-9=-27=(27)

-27-4=-31=(31)

Therefore, it is divisible by 31.

Hence solved.

Try with Both Methods

Let's try to check the divisibility of the same number using the positive and negative osculation processes.

Positive Process

 Check if 24836 is divisible by 7

or not using the positive osculation process.

 *Exercise 13.3*

Q1. Check the divisibility of the following.

1)   43721 by 51

2)   33324 by 41

3)   45423 by 91

4)   12342 by 53

5)   873622 by 27

WORKSHEET-16

Checking Divisibilit by Prime Numbers

Q1. Give the positive osculator of the following numbers :

1)	69 =	2)	99 =	3)	89 =
4)	7 =	5)	43 =	6)	139 =
7)	23 =	8)	31 =	9)	129 =
10)	37 =				

Q2. Give the negative osculator of the following numbers :

1)	71 =	2)	81 =	3)	11 =
4)	121 =	5)	41 =	6)	13 =
7)	37 =	8)	17 =	9)	7 =
10)	53 =				

Q3. Osculate the following numbers and test the divisibility :

1)	232 by 19 =	2)	3223 by 19 =	3)	3243 by 19 =
4)	32242 by 19 =	5)	22143 by 29 =	6)	54223 by 29 =

Vedic Maths

7) 331452 by 29 =   8) 224253 by 39 =   9) 425433 by 39 =

10) 2214452 by 49 =   11) 121523 by 49 =   12) 322242 by 59 =

13) 115322 by 59 =   14) 224324 by 59 =   15) 3312322 by 69 =

16) 2243523 by 69 =   17) 334231 by 79 =   18) 4322214 by 79 =

19) 3310233 by 79 =   20) 4213112 by 89 =   21) 84651 by 21 =

22) 43721 by 51 =   23) 404395 by 31 =   24) 42731 by 13 =